The Darts Bible

David Norton & Patrick Mcloughlin
with Steve Brown

CHARTWELL
BOOKS, INC.

This edition published in 2010 by
Chartwell Books, Inc.
A division of Book Sales, Inc.
276 Fifth Avenue Suite 206
New York, New York 10001
USA

ISBN-10: 0-7858-2601-7
ISBN-13: 978-0-7858-2601-9
QTT.DARB

A Quintet book
Copyright © Quintet Publishing Limited
All rights reserved.

This book was conceived,
designed, and produced by
Quintet Publishing Limited
The Old Brewery
6 Blundell Street
London N7 9BH
United Kingdom

Project Editors: Robert Davies, Martha Burley
Designer: Allen Boe
Illustrator: Stuart Holmes
Art Editor: Zoë White
Art Director: Michael Charles
Managing Editor: Donna Gregory
Publisher: James Tavendale

Printed in China

Acknowledgments
The authors wish to thank the following people for their
invaluable co-operation in the writing of *The Darts Bible*.
Steve Brown, Martin Adams, Dave Alderman (BDO),
Dave Allen (PDC), David Broughton (Unicorn), Dr
Patrick Chaplin PhD, Olly Croft (BDO), Steve Daszko,
Anastasia Dobromyslova, John Edwards (Winmau),
Ian Flack (Winmau), Della Fleetwood, Trina Gulliver,
Scott Harrison, Barry Hearn (PDC), Robert Holmes
(BDO), David King (Darts501.com), Paul Lim, Adam
Lane (Harrows), Richard Lowy (Unicorn), Stanley
Lowy (Unicorn), Steve Mottershead, Roisin O'Shea
(Winmau), John Part, Lee Peppard, Philippe Plouvier,
Roy Price (WDF), Robert Pringle (Harrows), Dennis
Priestley, Hayley Scott (PDC), Paul Seigel, George
Silberzahn, Phil Taylor, Raymond van Barneveld, Ed
van der Veer, Sid Waddell, and Alan Williamson Jr.

Picture Credits
Corbis 10 © Historical Picture Archive/CORBIS; 15 B ©
Hulton-Deutsch Collection/CORBIS; 151 © Bettmann/
CORBIS. **Fotolia** 97. **Getty Images** 6 John Gichigi/
ALLSPORT; 9 Tom Shaw/ALLSPORT; 15 A H. Allen/
Topical Press Agency/Getty Images; 27 David E.
Scherman/Time & Life Pictures/Getty Images; 68 Ian
Walton/Getty Images; 71 John Gichigi /Allsport; 110
MAX NASH/AFP/Getty Images; 116 © David Leahy;
117 ADRIAN DENNIS/AFP/Getty Images; 118 John
Gichigi/Getty Images; 127 General Photographic
Agency/Getty Images; 149 G. Adams/Stringer/Hutton
Collection; 154 Julian Herbert/Getty Images; 157 Julian
Herbert/Getty Images; 159 Paul Gilham/Getty Images;
163 Paul Gilham/Getty Images; 170 Paul Gilham/
Getty Images; 172 Christopher Lee/Getty Images;
174 Ryan Pierse/Getty Images; 176 Julian Herbert/
Getty Images; 178 MAX NASH/AFP/Getty Images;
180 Ian Walton/Getty Images; 182 Paul Gilham/
Getty Images; 184 Julian Herbert/Getty Images; 186
Julian Herbert/Getty Images; 188 MAX NASH/AFP/
Getty Images; 190 Donald Miralle/Getty Images; 192
Julian Herbert/Getty Images; 193 MAX NASH/AFP/
Getty Images; 194 Paul Gilham/Getty Images; 195 Paul
Gilham/Getty Images; 196 Jeff Gross/Getty Images;
iStock 2; 54; 94; 199. **Patrick Chaplin** 11; 13. **Rex
Features** 18 ITV / ITV Archive (618137tk); 19 Jason
Alden / Rex Features (845795a); 166 SPORTING
PICS / Rex Features (399175d); 168 CRISPIN
THRUSTON / Rex Features (399175n); 197 Steve
Bardens / Rex Features (722369g.) **Shutterstock**
17; 43; 74; 102; 125; 131; 162; 201; 203; 209.
Steve Brown 7; 88. **Unicorn Darts** 34; 37.
Winmau Dartboard Co. 44; 46; 47.

**"Gospel according to... Phil Taylor" pages are
taken from an exclusive interview between
the authors and Phil Taylor, 2009.**

Contents

Foreword

By Steve Brown
Two-times North American Open Champion

I will admit to being more than a little shocked—although deeply flattered—when I received the request to contribute to *The Darts Bible*, and I must thank my friends and colleagues for suggesting my name to the authors. What we have here is a remarkably comprehensive guide to our wonderful sport.

I know some of you may be wondering just who I am, and although never having quite reached "superstar" status (well, not yet, anyway!), I have achieved much success during my 30-plus years of competitive darts. That's a long time to be involved in any sport, and I am extremely proud of the fact that I have been competing internationally for well over twenty years.

One of the factors behind this success is the knowledge I have acquired from those around me, particularly my late father. Ken Brown was one of the first full-time professionals of the modern era, representing both England and Great Britain, and he was certainly my greatest influence. He was also known for what he put back into darts in a quest to help others, and nothing gives me greater pleasure than to do the same.

Of course, my contribution here is relatively minor, as there is much more to this project than just the basic mechanics and strategies of the game. However, these items should never be underestimated. At tournament level, they can make the difference between victory and defeat

and, as good as I am, I still win many matches as a result of strategy.

There have been many darts books published over the years, but nothing has ever come close to being all-encompassing—until now. Although I do fancy myself as something of a darts historian, my efforts pale in comparison to the tremendous efforts of those associated with this book. *The Darts Bible* will be an invaluable tool for all students of the game.

Above: Steve Brown (left) winning his first "Cockney Classic" competition in 1986. He was presented with the award by the world champion Eric Bristow (right).

Chapter One:
THE HISTORY OF DARTS

One of the stated aims of the World Darts Federation is "to gain Olympic recognition for the sport of darts." And yes, you did read that correctly. Darts has been officially recognized as a sport since 2005. Whether it deserves a place at the greatest sporting event on Earth is sure to spark debate, but what is beyond question is the global appeal of darts. Seventy countries are now affiliated with the WDF—its newest members as diverse as Nepal, Poland, and Serbia—and the sport's popularity in other parts of the world, particularly the Far East, is growing at an astronomical rate.

Ronnie Baxter
enters the arena
before his match
against Steve
Brown in the
quarter-finals
of the World
Matchplay
tournament
in 2000.

Origins of Darts

So the future looks bright for darts; but what of its history? The game first gained widespread popularity in the pubs of Victorian England, many of which have survived from the late nineteenth century to the early twenty-first. Spend time in any of these, talking to darts enthusiasts, and it will not be long before you hear a theory as to where the origins of the game lie. However most of these historical tales—that English soldiers played darts on the eve of the Battle of Agincourt in 1415, that King Henry VIII was given darts as a present by his future wife Anne Boleyn in 1531, that the Pilgrims played darts on the Mayflower as they sailed to America in 1620—are no more than urban myths.

A group of men practice their crossbow shooting at Penshurst Place, England, 1838. Although there is no evidence that darts developed from crossbow shooting, it has definitely been influenced by such traditional target games.

Similarly, there is no documented evidence to suggest that darts is an offspring of archery, or developed from shooting a bow and arrow or crossbow, although all these target games may have influenced darts. Instead, it would appear that darts were blown before they were thrown, in an English game called Puff and Dart that dates back to the sixteenth century. Hand-held darts similar to those used today almost certainly only originated in the mid-to-late nineteenth century in northern France, from where they were imported to Britain and the game as we know it today began to take shape.

Although it became the most popular of pub games, the appeal of darts was not confined to drinking establishments. It soon attracted not only hundreds of thousands of participants but also the attention of engineers who shaped its playing equipment, promoters who staged lucrative competitions, and, eventually, television companies whose interest gave rise to a professional game that now reaches across the world. Here, then, are the key events that shaped the history of darts.

1854

Anne Elizabeth Baker, in her *Glossary of Northamptonshire Words and Phrases*, describes Puff and Dart, the likeliest predecessor of darts, as "a game played by puffing or blowing a dart through a

Puff and Dart, a game from the 1850s.

long, narrow tube, aiming to strike numbers painted on a circular board hung against a wall; the various figures are arranged like those on the face of a clock and he who strikes the three highest numbers wins the game."

1881

Cassell's Book of Indoor Amusements, Card Games and Fireside Fun refers to a new indoor game, Dart and Target, in which darts are thrown, rather than blown, at a board with concentric circles and a central bullseye for different scores.*

MID- TO LATE NINETEENTH CENTURY

The earliest-known record of the French game *Javelot* appears. Players throw small javelins, which have feathered flights and are much longer and heavier than darts, at a target consisting of two rings. The target is smaller and farther away than in modern darts (see The Dart, pages 20–39). Each turn consists of two throws, rather than three, with one point scored for hitting the outer circle and two for the inner circle. *Javelot* is still played in northern France.

1880s

Mass production of cheap darts similar in shape and size to those used today begins in the village of Hasnon, near Lille, in northern France. Hasnon becomes the main source of darts for the British market until World War Two. By 1932, there are 30 different manufacturers in the village, producing 100,000 darts per day for export to Britain alone.*

*** Source: Played at the Pub, English Heritage.**

1885

The Perigueux family move to Manchester from northern France and begin the manufacture of wooden dartboards and darts under the name Perrigo. They produce Manchester Log-End boards, thought to be the forerunner of the "Clock" design board that is used today. The company continues to make darts equipment until 2003.

1898

An American inventor by the name of Nathan P. McKenney, from Dixon in the County of Lee, Illinois, patents the first folded paper flight. Before that—and for many years hence—they are made from feathers. Synthetic materials are first used for flights in 1945 and flights are now made from plastic, nylon, or polyester.

1903

A publication produced by the Licensed Victuallers' Gazette Office mentions both Puff and Dart and Dart and Target as "lawful games"

played in British pubs on a board of "concentric circles." Local darts leagues are introduced, often run by breweries, although the only evidence that remains from before the start of World War One in 1914 is of a league organized by Morland and Co., in Oxfordshire.

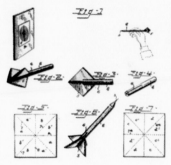

This drawing from the late nineteenth century depicts the first paper flight.

1913

Thomas William Buckle devises the numbering sequence that is still used for the Clock dartboard. Many sources erroneously claim that Brian Gamlin, a carpenter from Bury, England, thought up the numbering in 1896, but research by the darts historian Dr Patrick Chaplin suggests that Buckle, a Yorkshireman, deserves the credit. Interestingly, Buckle is said never to have taken out a patent for or explained the thinking behind his design.

1919

Englishman Ted Leggatt, an industrial chemist, invents an odorless modeling clay that is used as an alternative to wood in the manufacture of dartboards. The name given to his company—Nodor, derived from the words "no odor"—is still synonymous with the game. In 1935, Nodor launches the first bristle dartboard, made from sisal. Seventy-five years later, bristle dartboards are still by far the most commonly used in the game.

1924

The National Darts Association, the game's first governing body, is formed in Great Britain, in part because pubs, clubs, and breweries want to standardize the various regional versions of the game that have sprung up. The following year, the first rules of play are drawn up and the Clock dartboard is adopted as the standard board.

1927–8

The first News of the World Championship is staged in London and won by Sammy Stone. Sponsored by the Sunday newspaper of that name, it begins life as a regional event but grows steadily in popularity to become a national competition after World War Two. A crowd of more than 14,000 attends the 1939 final at the Royal Agricultural Hall in Islington, North London. For many years "the News of the World" is the most prestigious tournament in darts, and from

1970 it becomes the first to be televised annually. It is last played in 1997, when Phil Taylor wins the men's title.

1937

Frank Lowy, a Hungarian-born engineer, produces the first precision-made set of darts—The Silver Comet—which is sold in British shops. Lowy goes on to become the greatest pioneer in darts manufacture and his company, Unicorn, is responsible for many subsequent innovations, including the first copper and nickel silver darts (1939), the first flights to be made from plastic (1945), and the first darts to be classified and sold by weight (1949).

1962

Darts is broadcast on television for the first time. Westward TV, a regional channel, shows an invitational event in south-west England. It is another decade before the game enjoys widespread television coverage in the country.

Above: The Individual Darts Championship in 1936—organized by the National Darts Association.

Left: Men of the Indian Auxiliary Corps playing darts, 1940.

1970

The Southern California Darts Association organizes the first North American Open. Boasting total prize-money of $2,000, the event draws competitors from California, Oregon, Pennsylvania, and New Jersey. It continues until 1999, and is replaced on the calendar the following year by the Professional Darts Corporation's Las Vegas Desert Classic, the 2009 edition of which carries a total purse of $250,000. It is won by Phil Taylor.

1972

The most significant revolution in the modern history of darts manufacturing takes place as Unicorn produce the first commercial tungsten darts. The density of the metal allows for the darts to be made much thinner than a brass or nickel silver dart of the same weight and tungsten immediately becomes the preferred choice of professional players.

1973

Olly Croft founds the British Darts Organisation (BDO). Croft and other like-minded enthusiasts form a democratic organization to serve the game and its players. The BDO is run from the front room of Croft's house in north London. It becomes the recognized governing body for darts, and formulates the rules and guidelines by which the game is played throughout the world. In 2003, Croft is honored by being appointed OBE in the Queen's Birthday Honours List.

1974

The World Masters is staged for the first time and Englishman Cliff Inglis is crowned champion. Two years later Winmau, the world's leading dartboard manufacturer, begins its sponsorship of the event, which continues to the present day. The Winmau World Masters is one of two "major" tournaments sanctioned by the BDO; the 2009 edition attracts 400 players from 70 countries, with England's Martin Adams and Linda Ithurralde lifting the men's and women's singles titles.

1975

American Rudy Allison develops the electronic dartboard. Designed for use with soft-tip darts, the board features thousands of miniature holes in which the darts lodge and via which the score is recorded automatically. Soft-tip darts becomes widely played in the United States and parts of Europe and its popularity is increasing rapidly in the Far East. The same year sees the throwing distance for steel-tip darts standardized at 7 feet 9¼ inches (2.37 meters).

1976

The World Darts Federation (WDF) is formed by member organizations in 15 countries. It organizes a series of prestigious international competitions, including the World Cup, Asia-Pacific Cup, Americas Cup, and Europe Cup. The number of affiliated countries grows to 70 by 2009, with more than 350,000 players represented.

Above: An electronic dartboard— introduced in 1975.

From 1984 the WDF introduces a global ranking system, the first world

Above: Five-times world champion Eric Bristow on British TV series "Bullseye" in 1986.

No. 1 being the five-times world champion, Eric Bristow.

1978

Welshman Leighton Rees wins the inaugural BDO World Championship at the Heart of the Midlands Club in Nottingham, England. Featuring 16 competitors from eight countries, the tournament boasts a first prize of £3,000 (approx. $4,500), a modest sum compared with the £100,000

(approx. $150,000) that Englishman Martin Adams collects for winning the 2010 title. In 2001, the first BDO Women's World Championship is held and England's Trina Gulliver wins the first of eight world titles.

1994

Two years after the leading professional players break away from the British Darts Organisation to form the World Darts Council, later renamed the Professional Darts Corporation (PDC), the first PDC World Championship is staged at the Circus Tavern in Purfleet, England. In an all-English final Dennis Priestley defeats Phil Taylor to become the first man to win both versions of the world title. The PDC World Championship becomes the most prestigious individual competition in the game and in 2010 the total prize-money rises to £1 million (approx. $1.5 million), with £200,000 (approx. $300,000) for the winner.

2005

In January, the inaugural PDC Premier League commences, featuring the top eight players in the world. Phil Taylor goes through the first three seasons of competition unbeaten and tops the regular-season table in each of the first five years, winning the first four end-of-season finals before losing to fellow Englishman James Wade in the 2009 showpiece.

On June 3, the sports councils of Great Britain and Northern Ireland officially recognize darts as a sport. As part of the campaign to support the application by the British Darts Organisation, Martin Adams, the captain of the England darts team, wears a pedometer during the BDO World Championship to measure his physical exertions. It records that he walks a total of 33,310 paces during practice and the tournament—a total of just under 15¾ miles.

Martin "Wolfie" Adams, the captain of the England darts team in 2005, is pictured here with his trademark Wolfie darts.

Chapter Two:
THE DART

The dart has four components: the point, the barrel, the shaft, and the flight. The last of these may also include a flight-securing device. Steel-tip darts are generally made so that the point is attached to the barrel, but the shaft and flight are separate pieces. Soft-tip darts are identical except, as the name suggests, for the point, which is detachable and made of plastic for use on electronic dartboards. Players can experiment with different combinations of these components to build a dart that suits their game, which is easier than altering their style of throwing to suit a particular dart.

Tools of the trade:
Ronnie Baxter
holds his darts
as he prepares
to throw.

From Front to Back: The Basics

STEEL-TIP OR SOFT-TIP?

Steel-tip darts are used on bristle dartboards, which they penetrate, whereas soft-tip darts are used on electronic boards on which the plastic point lodges in one of several thousand small holes. Electronic bristle dartboards are also available for use with steel-tip darts, although these are less commonplace.

❶ POINT

In most steel-tip darts, the point is fixed to the barrel, but it is possible to buy darts with retractable points, designed so that if a dart strikes the wire that divides the scoring segments on the board, it will be pushed into the board by the barrel rather than bounce out. Soft-tip points screw into the barrel of the dart, making them easy to replace when they become bent or damaged. Screw-in steel-tip points are also available for people who play soft-tip and steel-tip darts.

❷ BARREL

The key component. The material used to make the barrel will determine the shape—and to an extent the price—of a set of darts. Brass, copper, and tungsten are the metals most widely used. Because brass and copper are relatively inexpensive they make cheaper darts than tungsten, but they are also less hardwearing and much less dense, so a tungsten dart of a certain weight will be much

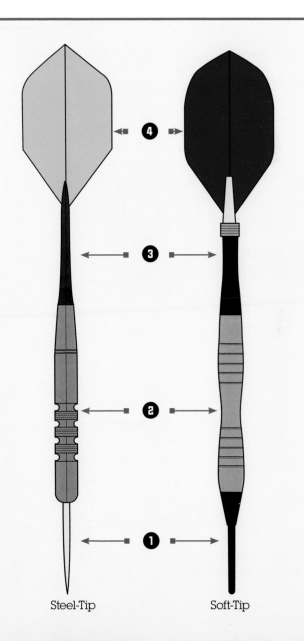

Steel-Tip   Soft-Tip

thinner than its brass or copper equivalent. This allows for better grouping (for example, three darts in the treble-20 bed), making tungsten the preferred choice of top players. It is used in alloys, most often with nickel, and the higher the percentage of tungsten, the higher the price of the darts will be. The size and shape of the barrel affect how a dart flies, but this is a matter of personal preference for the individual thrower, who should be primarily concerned with finding a barrel to suit their grip.

1969
Kirk Dormeyer, a New York stockbroker, wins the inaugural US Open Championship in his home city. There are no cash prizes on offer; instead successful players receive gifts.

❸ SHAFT

These are made in a variety of lengths from different materials including polycarbonate, nylon, and aluminum. It is also possible to buy spinning shafts. The advantage of these is that if a dart in the board is struck by a second one that is thrown, its flight should spin out of the way and the impact of any deflection will be reduced, as will the potential damage to the flight of the first dart.

❹ FLIGHT

The purpose of the flight is to provide lift force and keep the dart stable and traveling in the right direction. In general, the longer the dart, the greater the surface area of the flight should be, and the smaller the wings of the flight, the faster the dart will travel, so the key factors in determining the choice of flights are the style of the dart and the throw. Materials used for flights include plastic, nylon, dimplex, and polyester.

WEIGHT

Steel-tip darts can weigh up to 1¾ oz (50 g) but 1 oz (30 g) is considered fairly heavy by throwers and it is unusual to see darts above that weight. Soft-tip darts are much lighter—⅔ oz (18 g) or below—but in both forms of the game, finding the ideal weight is an individual decision best reached by trial and error, so it is advisable to start with darts of an average weight and go up or down according to experience and preference.

RULES

British Darts Organization rules governing the dimensions of the steel-tip dart state that it shall not exceed an overall length of 12 inches, nor weigh more than 1¾ oz (50 g). However, the vast majority of darts measure between 5 and 7 inches and most steel-tip players prefer weights from ⅔–1 oz (18–30 g) Soft-tip dartboards record scores electronically via circuits that are triggered by the point; therefore there is a weight restriction of ⅔ oz (18 g) per dart and a maximum length of 8 inches.

> ### 1970
> The North American Open Darts Tournament is staged for the first time in Culver City, Los Angeles, California. Vince Lubbering and Robbi Dobbs win the men's and women's singles titles.

Kevin Painter at the 2010 PDC World Championship.

Taking Shape: A History of the Dart

Just as there are more theories than there is evidence about the exact origin of the game itself, so mystery and myth surround the first darts. The arrow, the javelin, and the crossbow bolt are all claimed to be forerunners, but how or when any of these, which are used outdoors, inspired men to throw "arrows" at a target indoors is not documented.

Archery is the most likely of these three to be a forefather of darts, since many of the earliest dartboards used similar concentric targets and, of course, darts is also known as "arrows," especially in Britain. According to Dr Patrick Chaplin, the darts historian, the popular tavern game of "puff and dart," which dates back as far as the sixteenth century and in which small darts were blown at a board through a pipe rather than thrown, is also part of the game's bloodline.

However, the earliest evidence Chaplin has found of darts similar to those we see today is from the mid- to late nineteenth century. Imported to Britain from France chiefly for use in fairground games, these "French darts" were made from wood, with a sharpened metal point and turkey feathers acting as a flight. However, their lightness made them difficult to throw accurately, which put those playing the games at a disadvantage to those running them.

As darts grew in popularity, especially in British pubs, and became a game with proper rules, so its "tools of the trade" began to develop. To help improve accuracy, weight was added to wooden darts, most commonly in the form of a lead band. This led to the introduction of brass barrels, with a wooden spigot for a shaft. Although the first paper flight was invented in 1898, feathers remained popular for long after that.

Then in 1937 Frank Lowy, the founder of the Unicorn darts company, manufactured the first precision-made set of darts—the Silver Comet—and darts' technological revolution gathered pace. Soon, denser metals, including solid copper and nickel silver, were being used to make darts less bulky, and plastic flights were also introduced.

Cane and Brass darts.

Off-duty policemen enjoying a game of darts, London, England 1946.

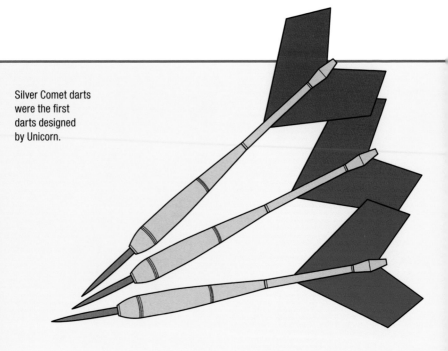

Silver Comet darts were the first darts designed by Unicorn.

1973
The appropriately named Ton Koster, of Holland, wins the first Dutch Open. The following year, female thrower Mary de Knoop upstages her male rivals to inherit Koster's crown.

In response to public demand for heavier or lighter models, darts began to be classified and sold by weight in the late 1940s. But arguably the greatest advance came in the 1970s, when tungsten darts were introduced. As tungsten is twice as dense as brass, such darts could be made considerably slimmer, giving players an advantage in tight scoring situations, such as trying to squeeze three darts into the treble-20 bed.

Another revolution followed in 1975, when soft-tip darts were introduced, allowing the game to be played on an electronic board that automatically recorded the score. The late 1980s saw titanium tungsten first used, and recent years have witnessed the employment of rarer metals such as rhenium.

Dart Production

The production of tungsten darts began in the early 1970s, when darts players who worked in engineering used welding rods to fashion their own darts from copper tungsten. Once these had been seen in competition, other leading players approached Unicorn and asked to have sets made for them, which the company was happy to do on an individual basis until the popularity of tungsten grew enough to persuade them to start commercial production.

Also known as Wolfram, represented in the periodic table by the letter "W," tungsten means "heavy stone" in Swedish. Although highly durable, in its natural state it is brittle and therefore is used in alloy form to make darts, most commonly with nickel.

The alloy will be heated to a temperature in excess of 5432°F before it is molded into long rods, or billets, that are then shaped into barrels by machine. Because the natural oils on a player's fingers will, in time, have a wearing effect on the barrel of a tungsten dart, it is common for a titanium coating to be applied, since titanium is impervious to such oils.

GOLDEN SHOT

In 1957, Frank Lowy and Unicorn Darts brought out the world's smallest dart,

The Golden Match (left) is the world's smallest dart.

the Golden Match, which measures just 2 inches and has 24-carat gold-plated barrels. Golden Match darts are still available and, because there is no restriction on the minimum size of a dart, can even be used in competition.

beam of light from the point of the dart on to the dartboard. The theory is that this will reveal any unsteadiness in the throwing arm and help the player to improve his alignment and aim.

STEADY IMPROVEMENT

One of the most recent innovations to help darts players improve their game has been the laser dart, a training tool that projects a

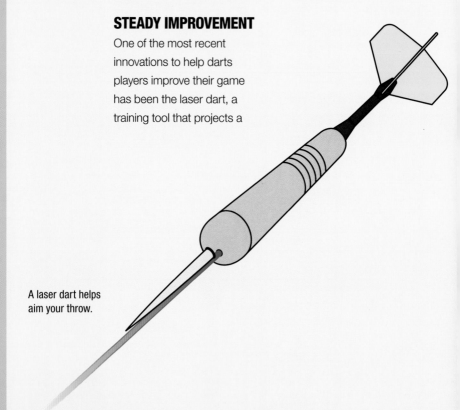

A laser dart helps aim your throw.

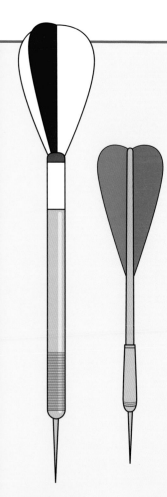

TOM THUMB

Introduced by Unicorn in 1946, this shorter-than-average dart was the result of early experimentation by the company's research team and featured a flight that had only two wings instead of the usual four. Although it was a striking design and performed as well as conventional darts, Tom Thumb never fully caught the imagination of the public. A "sibling" was also introduced, called Long Tom, which featured an extra-long shaft.

DUM-DUM DART

When it comes to darts of unusual shape and size, the Dum-Dum, designed in 1957, stands out because the weight of the dart is concentrated between the throwing fingers. Interestingly, because of this unique design, even if the Dum-Dum were thrown back to front it would turn around in mid air and enter the dartboard point first.

The Tom Thumb (above right), next to its "sibling," the Long Tom (left).

Dum-Dum darts (below) are weighted to turn themselves toward the board.

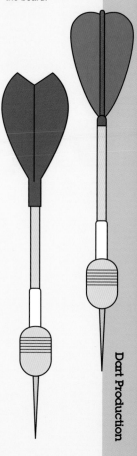

Dart Production

31

Above:
The Darrow

ARROWS TO DARROWS

Designed in 1953, the popular and eye-catching Darrow was inspired by the fletching on an arrow. The greater wing area made it fly more steadily through the air, but cleverly the flight did not appear to be larger when viewed from behind and therefore did not prevent close grouping of darts.

AROUND THE WORLD

In some countries, traditional versions of the game are still played that use very different darts than those we have come to regard as conventional. Flights made from turkey feathers are still used in American Darts, a regional variation of the game that originated in Pennsylvania and is still played there and in Delaware, Maryland, New Jersey, and New York State. The darts are made of wood and generally weigh between ⅓–½ oz (10–15 g).

In **Vogelpik**, which is said to have originated in Flanders around 300 years ago, the darts—or piks, as they are known—are made of wood, very light—in some cases as low as ⅕ oz (5 g)—and still have feathered flights. Because the target in Vogelpik is smaller than in darts, the piks are harder to throw accurately.

Javelot is another traditional game that has been played in northern France since the nineteenth century and provides more clues as to how the dart may have evolved. Players throw small javelins that are much longer and heavier than darts—12 to 16 inches in length and 9–14 oz (250–400 g) in weight—at a target that is farther away—19 to 26 feet—and much smaller than a dartboard, measuring only 8½ inches in diameter.

A more unusual distant relative of darts is **Struifvogel**,

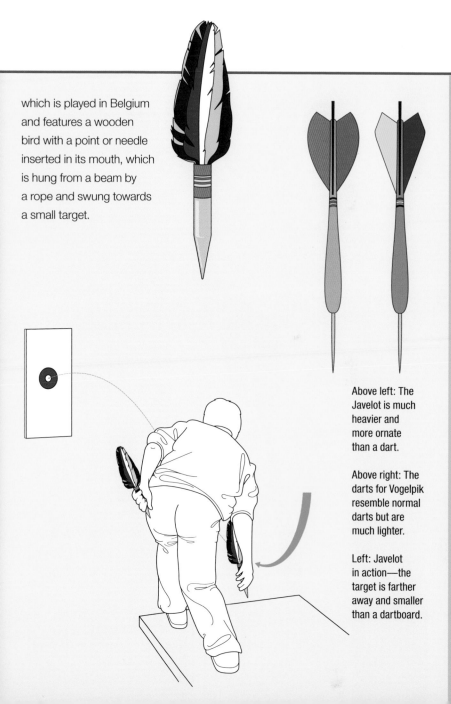

which is played in Belgium
and features a wooden
bird with a point or needle
inserted in its mouth, which
is hung from a beam by
a rope and swung towards
a small target.

Above left: The
Javelot is much
heavier and
more ornate
than a dart.

Above right: The
darts for Vogelpik
resemble normal
darts but are
much lighter.

Left: Javelot
in action—the
target is farther
away and smaller
than a dartboard.

The Appliance of Science

Since 1937, when Frank Lowy produced the Silver Comet, the first precision-made set of darts, there have been many technological advances.

The Uniboffin works with engineers at Unicorn's Research and Development department to assist Team Unicorn players with their individual dart development. Here, he explains the impact of the appliance of science:

"Although the barrel tends to be the component players focus on as it's the main part they have to hold and throw, from an aerodynamics perspective the design of the flights is really more significant. They act like a plane's wing and provide a lift force that straightens up the dart whenever it's flying at an angle. The amount of lift they produce obviously depends on their size and shape and without it the dart would just as happily fly sideways. As for the most effective material

A black Phase 5 dart, part of the Phil Taylor series from Unicorn, is equipped with a 100 percent titanium shaft to ensure a better grip.

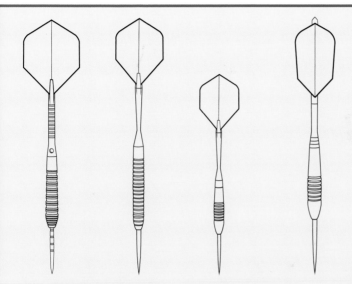

for flights, it could be argued that's natural feather, but polyester is more practical!

"The distance between the flights and the balance point [center of gravity or CG] of the dart is the lever arm the lift acts over, which is thus related to shaft length. The weight distribution of the barrel, shaft, and flights determines both the CG of the dart and its inertia to the straightening effect of the lift from the flights. A scientifically designed dart thus needs to combine

good barrel ergonomics with the right flights, shaft, and weight distribution.

"Barrels come in different shapes and sizes because people are different! It is crucial to a player's results that the barrel suits their individual throwing style. Unicorn's 'Sigma' darts assume a player has no strong preferences on barrel shape or grip. They can thus have, within the limits of practicality, a scientifically optimal weight distribution. This gives maximum scope

The size and shape of darts have evolved rapidly in recent years, although much is due to personal preference.

for designing specific shafts and flights which offer either extreme accuracy for the top-class player or a very 'forgiving' dart for the less skilled. I formulated the basic design for Sigmas many years ago, but at the time Unicorn felt the concept was too difficult to explain to the darting public and so the project was shelved until the advent of the internet allowed the idea to be described properly and interacted with using their website.

"Sigma darts are now a bestseller, helped by the design feature of the same in-flight performance being offered across a weight range. This is achieved by the unusual expedient of the heavier darts being shorter than the lighter ones, a factor that ensures the inertia stays comparable."

DARTS OF THE FUTURE

The Uniboffin sees a technical future for darts. "I don't think the aerodynamics of darts is going to change much, but I'm sure material technology will. I therefore see an increase in the use of advanced materials and manufacturing processes, perhaps leading to more shaft designs in composite plastics and exotic lightweight alloys and even barrels in exotic heavyweight alloys, as well as with hi-tech surface coatings. In general, I see a trend for genuine innovation as opposed to gimmickry. The darting public is becoming increasingly sophisticated and technology-savvy and thus able to tell the difference!"

1974
Darts' oldest major, the World Masters, is held for the first time. Sixty-five-year-old Belgian Andre Declerq reaches the last eight before Englishman Cliff Inglis lifts the trophy.

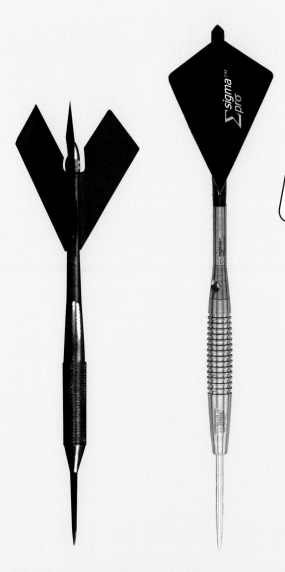

The Silver Comet from 1949 (left) was Unicorn's first ever dart. Contrasting it with the Sigma Pro from 2010 (right), shows how streamlined and lightweight the designs have become.

The Silver Comet, 1949

Sigma Pro, 2010

The Appliance of Science

Dart Regulations

Under BDO rules, players must provide their own darts and these should not exceed 12 inches in length or 1¾ oz (50 g) in weight each. The point of the dart must be fixed to the barrel and the rest can comprise three elements: a stem (or shaft); a flight; and a flight-securing device.

National Dart Association regulations for soft-tip darts state that the maximum length is 8 inches and the weight should not exceed ⅔ oz (18 g) although the latter may vary in areas. Tips must be detachable from the barrel and standard factory-issue for electronic darting, and should not be broken.

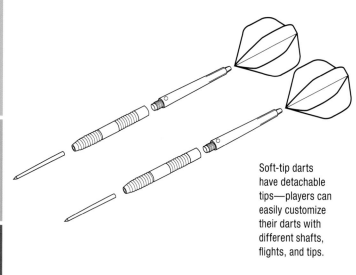

Soft-tip darts have detachable tips—players can easily customize their darts with different shafts, flights, and tips.

Tinkering

"I like to keep experimenting, to mix things up, change things. If you keep doing the same things over and over you get stale, so you've got to keep moving on.

"That's what I'm like, especially with my darts, you change things like flights and stems and barrels. I'm always thinking: 'What if I do this or change that?' It's good; it keeps things fresh.

"Unicorn are always working on how to produce a better version of the darts I use. I know they will come up with something that will be even better than the ones I have now. Alex Ross is the designer, he's the brains behind my darts and he's a genius. If I ask him to make something he just does it. Nine times out of ten it may not work but if I have any new ideas I tell Alex and say to him: 'Can you make them become reality?' Two days later, they're at my door.

"I was practicing one night and I picked up my wife Yvonne's darts, threw them, and liked them so much that I used them in a Premier League match against Wayne Mardle the following week and whitewashed him 8–0. Easy. I'm always changing and the best thing about it is that it does the other players' heads in."

Chapter Three:
THE DARTBOARD

The Clock board (also sometimes known as the London or Trebles board) has become the standard target for the game of darts. It is divided into scoring segments for the numbers 1 to 20 by a wire that is often referred to as the "spider." The sequence of numbers may appear to be random, but it is in fact uniform, starting with the 20 at the top (more of this later in the chapter). There is an outer ring for doubles, an inner ring for trebles, plus inner and outer bullseyes, worth 50 and 25 points respectively. Recognized the world over, the Clock board has been in existence for around a century, but it is strikingly different from the earliest dartboards and is an amalgamation of several regional variations that existed beforehand.

The Clock board
is now used
in all major
tournaments.

Dartboard History

The first dartboards were little more than cross-sections of tree trunks, on which the concentric rings were useful for measuring scores in a similar fashion to archery, and probably inspired the rings for doubles and trebles. Likewise, the cracks that appeared when the wood became dry or old may have led to the board being divided into scoring segments.

As the sport and its equipment began to take shape in the late nineteenth century, boards were still made from wood but became more sophisticated in design. Elm and poplar were the most popular materials but a significant drawback was that wooden boards needed to be soaked overnight in water when not in use. There were two reasons for this: to allow the holes made by darts to close up; and to prevent the board from becoming too hard or even splitting.

It was not until the early part of the twentieth century that other materials began to be used to manufacture dartboards. Modeling clay boards became popular but again, they were not without their disadvantages; they needed to be rolled flat from time to time and, more significantly, they gave off an unpleasant smell. A remedy to the latter problem emerged in 1919, when an Englishman called Ted Leggatt, an industrial chemist, invented an odourless modeling clay. Called Nodor (from "no odor"), the clay was soon used in the manufacture of dartboards, although the concept enjoyed limited success.

In 1935, Nodor produced a dartboard made from short

pieces of rope that had been laced vertically and then bound. The idea had been brought to the company four years earlier by Frank Dabbs, a publican from Kent, and was developed by Leggatt before the two men patented the idea. Nodor's creation was called "The Original Bristle" and a key attraction was that the holes created by darts closed once the darts were removed. Bristle dartboards remain the most popular of all. The best modern-day bristle boards are made from sisal, a fiber that is used to make ropes, often sourced in East Africa.

Some companies continued to manufacture boards made from other materials. At the cheaper end of the market boards made from compressed paper coils were popular. Elm boards remained in production in Great Britain until the 1970s, when a severe outbreak of Dutch Elm

Disease brought about their demise. The same decade also saw the introduction of soft-tip darts and electronic boards. The latter were designed with several thousand small holes to accommodate the darts and automatically recorded the scores as each one landed.

Dartboards have come a long way since they were cross sections of tree trunks—personal varieties are still easy to come by though.

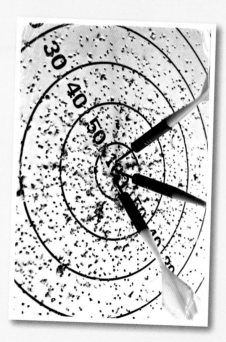

Manufacture

HOW IS A DARTBOARD MANUFACTURED?

John Edwards, operations director of Nodor, explains how Winmau dartboards are made, a process that begins in the plant world.

1) Bristle dartboards are made using fibers from the sisal plant, which is native to countries in North and South America, Africa, and the Far East. Brazil, Tanzania, Kenya, and China are the world's leading producers. A cactus-leaf plant, sisal has fleshy, sword-shaped leaves that grow three to six feet in length and contain long strands of fibers that are used in the production of ropes, twine, and dartboards.

Winmau, the leading

manufacturer of dartboards, uses sisal only from Kenya, in East Africa, where it has been farmed extensively since the nineteenth century. Kenyan sisal has been used for about that length of time by the British Navy to make marine ropes. It is cleaner and whiter in appearance than sisal found in other parts the world.

2) The first step in the manufacture of a dartboard is to separate the sisal fibers from the leaves of the plant. This is done by a machine process called decortication, in which the leaves are crushed and beaten. The fibers that remain account for only 5 percent of the total plant and it will take one ton of sisal leaves to make ten dartboards.

3) After decortication, the fibers are washed and dried before being drawn out and combed by machine into a sliver, an interwoven thread of fibers with a uniform consistency of length and thickness (see image opposite). The slivers are then made into bales measuring about 3 inches in diameter, each one containing hundreds of thousands of individual fibers on end.

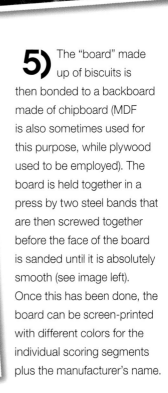

4) Another machine then cuts the bales into biscuits—cross-sections of the bale measuring 4 to 5 inches in diameter and 1¼ inches in thickness (see image, right). These are wrapped in paper or tape around their outside edge. Around 50–60 of these biscuits will then be compacted into the shape of the dartboard. Each board will therefore have millions of fibers.

5) The "board" made up of biscuits is then bonded to a backboard made of chipboard (MDF is also sometimes used for this purpose, while plywood used to be employed). The board is held together in a press by two steel bands that are then screwed together before the face of the board is sanded until it is absolutely smooth (see image left). Once this has been done, the board can be screen-printed with different colors for the individual scoring segments plus the manufacturer's name.

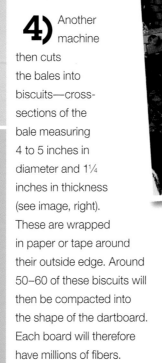

The Dartboard

6) The final stage in the production process sees the addition of the wires. Some cheaper boards use a welded, one-piece wire, but all Winmau boards use individual wires, which makes the structure less rigid. First the concentric rings—the bull, doubles, and trebles—are driven in before the radial wires are individually placed and pressed by machine. Finally the numbers are added and the dartboard is ready for use.

The Clock Board

THE BASICS

The Clock board is the most familiar of all dartboards—here is an explanation of how the board works.

❶ DOUBLES RING

The outer scoring ring of the board. Any dart that lands here scores twice the number of that segment. Most -01 games must be finished by scoring on a double.

❷ TREBLES RING

The inner scoring ring lies between the two single-scoring segments. A dart landing here scores three times the number of that segment (i.e. a treble 20 scores 60 points).

❸ INNER BULLSEYE

A dart landing here scores 50. In -01 games, players can finish by hitting the inner bullseye, which effectively counts as a double 25.

❹ OUTER BULLSEYE

A dart that lands here scores 25. However, a player cannot finish a "doubles out" -01 game by hitting the outer bullseye.

❺ SINGLE SCORING

The two segments either side of the trebles ring; a dart that lands here scores the number of that segment.

❻ OUT OF PLAY

Any dart that lands in the area outside the doubles ring does not score and cannot be thrown again.

The Numbers Game

Why the numbers on a dartboard are arranged in the order they are is something of a mystery. A common myth is that Brian Gamlin, an Englishman from Bury, Lancashire, who was a carpenter by trade, devised the system in 1896 but died in 1903 before he could patent his design. However, exhaustive research by David King, the darts writer, and Patrick Chaplin, the darts historian, has uncovered no official record of Gamlin.

According to Chaplin, the man most likely to have thought up the numbering was Thomas William Buckle, an English craftsman from Dewsbury, West Yorkshire. Buckle is claimed to have produced the first "1–20" board in 1913, developing a Fives board, which has 12 segments, into one with 20 segments. How Buckle, or anyone else, came up with the arrangement of numbers one can only guess, but what is beyond dispute is that the design works perfectly for the game of darts.

Had the target remained a series of concentric rings, as in archery, good players would have been able to score bullseyes at will. Instead, high numbers are flanked by low ones—for example, 5 and 1 sit to the left and right of 20, 7 and 3 either side of 19, etc—increasing the risk element and demanding greater skill. Even a simple game such as Round the Clock, in which players must hit each number from 1 to 20, is made more

challenging by the layout.

Whoever came up with system is unlikely to have calculated it at the time but, ignoring the rule that the 20 must be at the top of the board, there are 121,645,100,408,832,000 permutations for the sequence of numbers on a board.

The order of the numbers is perfect—high scores are flanked by low scores so even the best players can be caught out.

Manchester Log-end Board

Wooden dartboards are still made and used in Manchester, England, where the game has been played since the nineteenth century on a log-end board. This unique board is black, much smaller than the Clock board, has no trebles ring and a thinner doubles ring, and its numbers are arranged in a sequence that is thought by some to be the original order.

The company that first manufactured the log-end board, Perrigo, ceased production in 2003, but the Manchester Log-End Federation, led by John Gwynne, the journalist and television commentator, persuaded David Mealey, a local craftsman, to take over the manufacture of the boards. "We have about 10,000 players in our local leagues in and around Manchester so I believe the log-end is the second most used board in existence," Gwynne says. "The boards are made of poplar these days, rather than elm. They still need to be soaked for 24 hours after they have been used [for the holes to close up] and kept in a sealed plastic bag to retain moisture until they are taken out for use."

Interestingly, Perrigo, the firm that originally made the log-end board, was founded by a French family who moved to Manchester in the nineteenth century and are thought to have brought the design with them, offering further evidence that the game of darts originated in France.

The Manchester
log-end board
features the
numbers in a
different order to
the Clock board.

Electronic Dartboards

The soft-tip dartboard, invented in 1975, was the brainchild of Rudy Allison, an American who had played the game for the first time while on holiday in Ireland and decided it would be improved if the scores could be recorded automatically. There are two main types of electronic

There are 9,776 scoring holes on the face of the Harrows Electro 180— a typical electronic dartboard.

board, or target, as it is called in soft-tip darts: machines that are coin-operated for use in pubs, bars, and public places; and home machines that are smaller, cheaper to buy, and free to play.

Robert Pringle, of Harrows Darts, explains how the boards work. "The face of the dartboard is basically a honeycomb of small holes, made from injection-molded plastic," he says. "Behind each hole there is a sensor pad, so when the tip of a dart penetrates the hole, it depresses the sensor, which triggers the memory and records the score. Soft-tip darts have points made of plastic that is slightly softer than the board, which helps the dart to penetrate the board."

In recent years, the same technology has been used to produce bristle dartboards, for use with steel-tip darts, that keep score automatically.

"Each bed is individually sensed," says Pringle. "There have also been experiments with an invisible laser-style grid covering the board, although there have been difficulties with this and research is continuing."

When electronic boards were first introduced, the dimensions of the beds for doubles and trebles were the same as for bristle dartboards. In the United States, manufacturers soon realized that increasing the size of these would speed up play by enabling players to record higher scores and finish more quickly, which is why they are slightly larger on some boards.

An advantage of electronic dartboards is that they can record scores for up to eight players at once and are programmed with a wide variety of games other than straight scoring (see "Fun and Games," pages 124–147).

Historical Boards

Before the Clock board became accepted as the standard target, dartboards varied from region to region in Great Britain. Indeed, it was estimated in 1914 that there were as many as 20 regional variations. Most of these have now disappeared but some survive and are still used. Here are some of the most popular designs:

CLOCK BOARD

The most commonly used board and the only one that is allowed in official competitions under BDO rules.

MANCHESTER LOG-END BOARD

Smaller than a standard board, it measures just 10 inches in diameter and is the only board that is still made from wood. There is no trebles ring, the doubles ring is thinner than on a Clock board, and the numbering is also different, with 4 situated at the top of the board and only 19 and the inner and outer bulls in the same position.

MAN-LON LOG-END BOARD

A hybrid of the Manchester log-end board and the conventional London or Clock board. It is the same size as the former, but the same style as the latter, with a trebles ring and the numbers in "conventional" order. The board is, however, frowned upon by those who still play on the original Manchester board.

YORKSHIRE BOARD

This is the board that Thomas William Buckle is said to have designed in 1913, the obvious difference between it and the Clock board being the absence of a trebles ring and a single bullseye, rather than an inner and outer. The board is still used in parts of the UK.

BURTON OR STAFFORDSHIRE BOARD

A variation on the Yorkshire board that is identical except for two 1-inch square boxes—situated between the numbers 14 and 9 and 4 and 13 on the wire—that counted as 25 if hit.

THE TONBRIDGE BOARD

This was unusual because the outside ring counted for trebles, while a small triangular section just inside the treble on each number from 1 to 20 counted for doubles, making finishing even trickier than usual.

BLACK IRISH BOARD AND LINCOLN BOARD

Both all-black variations of the Yorkshire board that differed only in that the Black Irish board was of conventional size while the Lincoln had a larger target area of 15 inches in diameter.

GRIMSBY BOARD

One of the most unusual designs, this had numbers from 1 to 28, with 28 at the top of the board and 20 relocated to about 10 o'clock. It is quite possible that the pairs of circles positioned just outside the target area at the four compass points were also scoring areas.

LONDON FIVES OR NARROW FIVES

The Fives version of the game is still played in parts of London, but because it only features round numbers —5, 10, 15, and 20—straight-scoring games such as 501 and 301 have to be changed to 505 and 305.

WIDE FIVES OR IPSWICH FIVES

Identical to the London Fives board except that the doubles and trebles rings are wider.

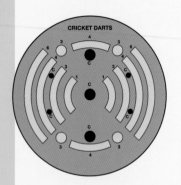

NOVELTY BOARD: CRICKET

Not to be confused with the popular points-scoring game of American Cricket, this is a very well thought-out attempt to recreate the English national game, in which, much like the sport itself, it is easier to score nought, one, or two than hit fours or sixes and take wickets.

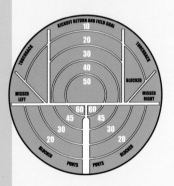

NOVELTY BOARD: AMERICAN FOOTBALL

This board, the design of which incorporates a set of American football posts, makes it possible to advance by yards down the field but offers a distinct advantage to players who are adept at throwing for the bullseye.

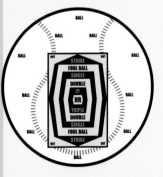

NOVELTY BOARD: BASEBALL

The thrower becomes a pitcher here: a clearly defined rectangular area of the board represents the strike zone and anything landing outside that area counts as a ball. Home runs are hard to hit and, of the many baseball dartboards, this is one of the best designs.

NOVELTY BOARD: GOLF

Many boards have attempted to recreate golf on a dartboard and this almost psychedelic effort features nine holes. The chapter "Fun and Games" (see pages 124–147) explains how golf can also be played on a conventional board.

NOVELTY BOARD: CARDS

All manner of games can be played on this board, which is divided into 52 segments (one for each card in the pack) plus an inner and outer bull that may represent the two jokers.

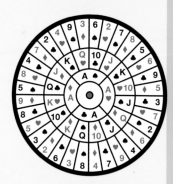

NOVELTY BOARD: SNOOKER

One of the simpler designs, this represents the table as it is set up for the start of a frame of snooker, and requires players to hit different colored balls in order to pot them.

Regulations

British Darts Organisation rules decree that the dartboard should be of the bristle variety and the 1–20 clock pattern, with the 20 at the top of the board, an inner ring for trebles, an outer ring for doubles, and inner and outer bulls scoring 50 and 25 respectively. The wires forming the "spider" that divides the scoring segments must be fixed to the board and lie flat on its face and the board must be fixed to the wall so that the center of the bull is 5 feet 8 inches from the floor. In soft-tip darts, the board is at exactly same height.

The National Dart Association in America recognizes boards with a target area of 15½ inches in diameter, but soft-tip boards with a target area of 13½ inches are also popular. The biggest difference is that on all soft-tip dartboards the doubles and trebles are fatter and easier to hit.

Raymond van Barneveld at the 2010 PDC World Championship in London. Van Barneveld was runner-up in 2009, but lost to Mark Webster in a third-place play-off in 2010.

■ Outside edge of "double" wire
to center bull: 169.8–171.2 mm

■ Outside edge of "treble" wire
to center bull: 104.8–105.2 mm

■ "25" ring inside
diameter: 31.8–32.2 mm

■ "Bull" inside
diameter: 12.5–12.9 mm

■ "Double" and "treble" rings inside width: 7.8–8.2 mm

■ Overall dartboard diameter: 448–454 mm

Regulations

63

LIGHTING

For tournament play, there are rules governing the lighting of the board. The minimum requirement is a suitably positioned light of 100-watt intensity, normally a spotlight hung from the ceiling that shines directly onto the board. This requirement is doubled to 200 watts for matches taking place on stage, while additional lighting is used for televised matches.

Outside stage and television events, however, shadows can still be a problem for the players. Scott Harrison, of Austin, Texas, USA, tackled this difficulty in 2004 when he invented the Circumluminator™), which encircles the board with light and completely eliminates shadows. Naturally, it is made of unbreakable material to cope with mis-thrown darts.

Lights should be positioned on the ceiling to avoid shadows which can distract.

Phil Taylor

Staying At The Top

"Persistence has kept me at the top for so long. I've seen players come and win a World Championship or a major title and immediately think that they've made it. I've seen them look through the tournament draw, and say: 'I've beaten him so I should get through to the next round. I've also beaten the guy in the next round so I should get through that as well.' And I think: 'What are you on about? This guy has qualified, he's a decent player; you can't think past him.'

"You just can't go into any competition thinking of past victories. I go in thinking I'm going to face the best player in the world ever and I won't take him for granted. Every player can pull a game out of the hat, so I don't care how good or bad someone is, I'll be ready for them.

"The way I approach things is to think that I've not won anything. When you ask me how many World Championships, World Matchplays, Desert Classics I have won, I wouldn't have a clue. I wouldn't have a clue how many records I've broken because they don't mean anything to me at this moment. I'm looking to the future. I'm getting ready for the next week. It's relentless."

Setting Up Your Own Dartboard

• The board must be hung so that the center of the bullseye is 5 feet 8 inches above a point on the floor that is level with where the player stands. Players throw from behind a toe-line or oche, which should be a raised bar measuring 2 feet in width and 1½ inches in height. Sometimes a mat clearly marking the throwing distance or a metal strip screwed into the floor is used, but for competitions a raised oche is preferred. A player may lean over the oche when throwing but must keep both feet behind the toe-line.

• The throwing distance measures 7 feet 9¼ inches from the back of the oche or throwing line to the face of the board. For soft-tip darts this distance is extended to 8 feet.

• As a further check, the diagonal measurement from the bullseye to the oche should be 9 feet 7⅜ inches for steel-tip darts. This is a useful way of determining whether the throwing area is on a level surface.

• Women throw from the same distance as men under BDO rules, but in a small number of local competitions the distance may be reduced to 7 feet 6 inches.

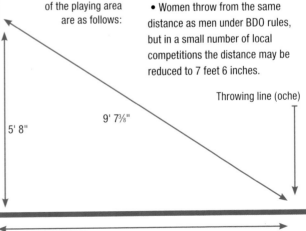

The standard dimensions of the playing area are as follows:

Throwing line (oche)

9' 7⅜"

5' 8"

7' 9¼"

GOING THE DISTANCE

Although the measurements for the throwing area are simple, this has not always been the case. When darts was in its infancy in Great Britain, the throwing distance varied according to region, from as little as 6 feet to 9 feet. When national tournaments were first played, a campaign began to settle on a universal measurement. In 1954, the National Dart Association set the distance at 7 feet 6 inches, but regional variations persisted and it was not until 1977 that the World Darts Federation and British Darts Organisation agreed on 7 feet 9¼ inches, which is still used today. It is worth noting this is a minimum distance and a player can throw from farther away if he or she chooses. A player may also throw from left or right of the oche as long as they stay behind the line. Despite this, in Manchester, England, where the log-end board is still used, the bullseye is 5 feet 3 inches off the ground and the throwing distance is 7 feet 6 inches.

OCHE OR HOCKEY?

Not only are there are many theories as to why the oche is so called, there is some dispute as to whether the original word was hockey rather than oche. One story suggests that, in parts of England, the throwing distance was first measured by placing crates from a brewery called Hockey & Sons end to end, hence the phrase "toeing the hockey." However, no record of the brewery has been found. The word "oche" is Flemish in origin and means "notch," while there is also an old English word, "hocken" that means "to spit." Given that the English phrase "spitting distance" means close proximity, it is quite conceivable that oche derives from hocken.

Phil Taylor

Preparation

"I look back at when I was younger and it frightens me when I think how much I practiced. I used to play county darts and be in The Crafty Cockney pub at nine in the morning before even the cleaners had come in. Sometimes I'd be on stage playing at five or six in the evening and I'd still be practicing up until when the game started. I wouldn't sit down once.

"I now only need to practice for about two hours per day. I've done the groundwork. You reach a stage where you look at how opponents

Phil Taylor celebrates winning a leg against Raymond van Barneveld during the final of the 2007 World Darts Championship.

practice and perform and you think: 'They won't beat me, not a chance, no way.' I'm too dedicated—and I mean dedicated.

"When I'm playing I try not to think too much about a match the night before. I make sure I get to the hotel I'm staying at in good time and get to bed early. Then I get up early, have breakfast, and maybe go out for a stroll. When I come back I have a short nap, shower, and change, and then I'm ready for anything. I only practice now for two hours before I go on.

"Sometimes I get criticized for not enjoying myself enough, get told I'm too serious, and I think: 'Yeah,

of course I am.' Like in Las Vegas, I'm up at 5am to follow my routine, but it makes me feel like I'm ready, and preparing properly is key.

"Some players go away to tournaments and want to go out every night. They used to slate me because I didn't want to go out nightclubbing or wherever they wanted to go, but I had a young family to feed when I got back. They could go back and their partner might say: 'Have you won?' They'd say: 'I got beat in the second round.' And she would say: 'Oh, never mind then.' I couldn't do it. No way could I go home and say I'd lost. I just couldn't do it week after week."

Chapter Four: THE THROW— A Steve Brown Masterclass

One of the beauties of darts is that, unlike most sports, it can be played by men or women, young or old, short or tall. In that sense, everyone starts on an equal footing, but for those who are just beginning to play the game, it is important to learn how to do the basics well. In this chapter Steve Brown, the only American male to be inducted into both the North American and Canadian Halls of Fame, presents a step-by-step guide to throwing that works for the complete novice or the seasoned player in need of a refresher.

Steve Brown
at the PDC
World Darts
Championship
in 1999.

Choosing Your Darts

The first thing a new player needs to do is buy their own set of darts, but with so many sizes, shapes, and styles available on the market, it can be difficult to know where to start. However, that needn't be the case, and the important thing is to start somewhere; there will be plenty of time for fine-tuning later, as Steve explains.

"Many people make the mistake of thinking that the more they pay for a set of darts, the better the darts will be. But just because you buy darts endorsed by Phil Taylor doesn't mean you'll start playing like Phil Taylor. My recommendation is that if you're starting out, you should buy what you can afford, even if it's just a cheap brass set, and then develop the mechanics of your throw, such as the grip and the release, which we'll come to later.

"In one respect, buying a set of darts is a bit like choosing a set of golf clubs.

You can't just look at a set of expensive clubs and assume they will feel right. With darts, the trick is to find a set that you're comfortable playing with, so head to a darts shop and try a few out. That's essential because what works for one person doesn't necessarily work for another; we're all different, our hands are different shapes and sizes, and our arms and bodies are all different.

"Of course, it's true that the combination of the barrel, shaft, and flight will affect how a dart flies, but these elements are all a matter of personal preference.

"Someone else may throw your darts and then tell you they're not balanced. Well, in my book there's no such thing. The truth may be that they're not correctly balanced for the way you throw. For example, I can't throw John Lowe darts, which have a shorter barrel than standard, as they're just not suited to my style. So find the dart that feels best to you.

"I use ¾ oz (20 g) Steve Brown darts made from nickel-tungsten. They are straight-barreled and what are important to me are the length and the weight, as well as the grip, but again this is a matter of personal preference. Most top professionals will have a dart designed to their own specifications, depending on the way they hold and throw the dart. Then, you choose the combination of flights/shafts that you feel comfortable with. The main things to look

for are not just accuracy, but also the way they fly through the air, and the way they land in the board; you should look for consistency here.

"Finally, don't be blinded by science. I know of companies that claim to make the 'most accurate darts in the world,' but is there really such a thing? Darts will not make you a good player—only you can do that!"

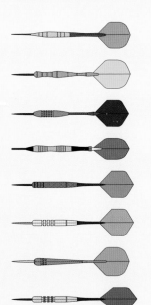

Darts are varied and it is best to try out many before you find your personal favorite.

Shapes and Sizes

Barrels are shaped, knurled, and grooved to suit different grips. While the choice may appear bewildering to the beginner, the good news is that there's something for everyone on the market.

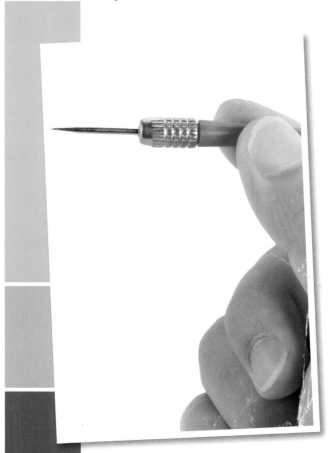

Watch and learn

"If you look at professional darts players, you'll see that most have a fairly similar grip, with the dart usually held between the thumb and forefinger, although the position of the thumb can vary quite a bit. The other fingers serve to keep the dart in position in the hand, and to stabilize the dart as it leaves the hand."

"Of all the factors in darts, the dart itself is the most personal, and the physical attributes of the individual are the key. It's not just the weight of the dart that's important, but also the length, diameter, shape, and grip.

"Our fingers are all different shapes and sizes, and the sensitivity of the fingers can vary greatly. It really is down to the individual as to what feels best, and there is no way that I, or anyone else, can say what is best for a player."

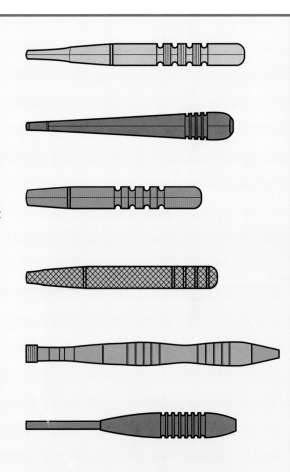

There are numerous barrel shapes to choose from, right.

The Stance

If you watch a darts match or a professional tournament and look closely at the individual players, you will almost certainly notice subtle differences about each one's stance. Some may stand sideways on; others may be more straight on. But which one is the best and what difference does it make how or where you align yourself?

Andy Hamilton throws at the 2010 PDC World Championship. His stance is completely untwisted.

"I would always suggest standing on the line with the leading foot and shoulder in line with the center of the board. It makes far more sense to stand centrally rather than way off to the left or right of the target. You wouldn't do that in archery or shooting, so why do it in darts?

"As for different approaches such as sideways on or straight on, that's all personal preference. Whatever feels comfortable is usually best, although you do need to feel that it doesn't compromise the accuracy and control of the dart at all.

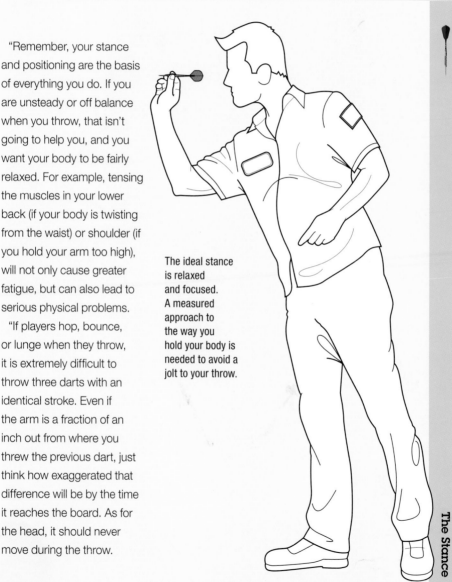

"Remember, your stance and positioning are the basis of everything you do. If you are unsteady or off balance when you throw, that isn't going to help you, and you want your body to be fairly relaxed. For example, tensing the muscles in your lower back (if your body is twisting from the waist) or shoulder (if you hold your arm too high), will not only cause greater fatigue, but can also lead to serious physical problems.

"If players hop, bounce, or lunge when they throw, it is extremely difficult to throw three darts with an identical stroke. Even if the arm is a fraction of an inch out from where you threw the previous dart, just think how exaggerated that difference will be by the time it reaches the board. As for the head, it should never move during the throw.

The ideal stance is relaxed and focused. A measured approach to the way you hold your body is needed to avoid a jolt to your throw.

James Wade
throws at the
2010 PDC World
Championship.
The placement
of his feet echoes
Stance C,
below right.

"Sometimes, a player may have to move, for example if they are aiming for a target that is blocked by another dart and need to change the angle of throw.

"Some players are more adept at the art of moving than others, but generally players move when they feel their shot is blocked. Naturally, changing target is an option, but many of us prefer to use the darts already in the board to our advantage. If, for example, you throw two darts on the outside wire of a double, you can—depending on their angle—move a little, and simply aim straight at those darts. If the third dart hits them, the chances are it will deflect into the double. In effect, you are actually making the target 'bigger.'

"My darts usually land flat, and even shooting for the treble 20, moving can be to my advantage. If my first dart lands right under the treble, I will often move to the side, and 'drop' the next dart on top, and into the treble. The ability to do this relies on one's own accuracy, and more importantly, how one's darts fly and land. That's why consistency is of paramount importance. If every dart flies and lands differently, there is no way to do this."

STANCE A

"This is a basic stance. The player may feel more comfortable putting a little more weight on the front foot. This can help reduce the tendency to rock or lunge during the stroke."

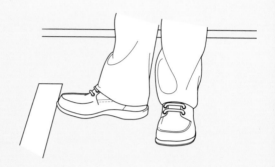

STANCE B

"Although common, this is not a position I would recommend. This increases the tendency of the player to 'hook' the dart to the left of the intended target. The angle and position of the feet is fine, but would probably be better from a more central position on the oche."

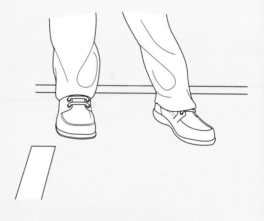

STANCE C

"A very common stance, with most of the weight on the front foot. The angle of the front foot to the oche makes it a much more natural position for throwing the dart, reducing tension in the back and shoulder. Everything (foot, hips, shoulder) is more in line with the target."

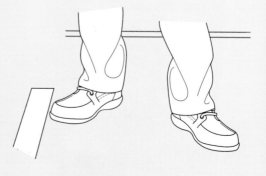

The Stance

Get a Grip

John Lowe, three times a world champion, is acknowledged as having a near-perfect grip: thumb under the barrel, index finger opposite, and middle finger resting on the end of the barrel. Eric Bristow, who won five world titles, raised the little finger on his throwing hand but admitted later in his career that this was just an affectation. So how exactly should you hold your darts? Although there is no right answer, it's important to get this right.

"As I said at the start, the grip should be natural and comfortable; don't try to 'manufacture' one. Just pick up a dart and throw it. Sure, people say I make it look easy, but I am just picking up an object, and I'm throwing it at the wall; what is easier than that?

"While it may be true that there is no right or

Ronnie Baxter's dart is pinched between the thumb and forefinger, and is stabilized by the other fingers. Here he throws at the 2010 PDC World Championship.

wrong way to throw a dart, there are certainly better and worse ways!

"Many players—and not usually the better ones—hold the dart with their very fingertips, but when I ask them, 'Where is the most feeling in your fingers?' the usual response is, 'The fingertips!' Many of you reading are thinking the same thing, right? Just reach out and pick up a glass, a pill bottle, a TV remote, or a cellphone. Now look; you're not using the fingertips, are you? You're using the pads of your fingers, and it's the pads that will give you more control of your darts.

"If you do happen to be one of those who holds the dart with their fingertips,

The pads of the fingers are the best places to hold a dart. Avoid using your fingertips as this gives you less stability.

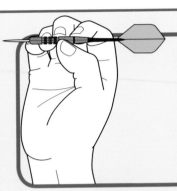

FINGERTIP GRIP

"Very common, particularly in the United States. The main problem here is that it can drastically reduce the ability to follow-through fully and smoothly. The dart is simply released as the fingers open, rather than being 'thrown.'"

STEVE BROWN GRIP

"Similar to those of many other top players, the barrel is basically pinched between the thumb and forefinger, and is stabilized by the other fingers. The dart leaves the hand almost parallel to the floor, and the release allows the wrist to roll or snap, and the arm will extend fully into a smooth follow-through."

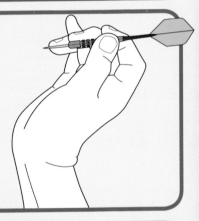

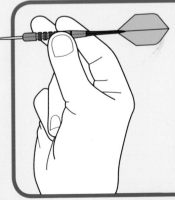

TWO-FINGERED GRIP

"Often touted as a recommended grip, the main problem with this grip is that the dart is held comparatively loosely; the dart moves very easily in the hand, leading to a tentative and inconsistent release. Also, the fact that the last two fingers are invariably drawn down into the palm of the hand can increase muscle tension in the palm, which can lead to an erratic release."

try using the pads. I can hear you saying, 'But it doesn't feel natural!' That's because instead of starting out with a natural grip, you 'manufactured' a grip, and took something unnatural and developed it into something that now feels natural to you.

"A truly 'bad' grip will cause a total lack of consistency in the release of the dart.

"What you are looking to achieve with the grip, basically, is a consistent and effective way not only to hold but also to release the dart. It's no good if you really don't have a clue what the dart is going to do when it leaves your hand, and it's surprising just how important the feel of a good release is. Experienced players can feel just how well, or how badly, they have thrown the dart, as soon as it leaves their hand. Sometimes, the dart leaves your hand, and you know that it's going exactly where you want. Pity we can't do that all the time..."

James Wade, throwing at the 2010 PDC World Championship. This image shows his alignment perfectly.

The First Throw

Once you are equipped with your darts—and the flights have been inserted—you are ready to play. But what is the best way for a beginner to approach the concepts of stance, grip, and throwing action? First things first: relax!

"Mechanically, darts is—or should be—a very simple game. You are not a baseball pitcher trying to pitch a fastball. Nor are you a basketball player trying to score from a free throw. Finally, the object you are holding is neither a pen nor a pencil, and you are certainly not attempting to write with it. You are merely trying to throw a small, and relatively light metallic projectile ($\frac{2}{3}$–1 oz/18–30 g, usually) at an 18-inch disk on the wall, from a distance of just under 8 feet.

"Try not to complicate matters; keep it simple and natural. If you've never thrown a dart before that's fine. Imagine that I've given you a ping pong ball (or you could always try this, if you have a ping pong ball at hand!), and I've asked you to throw it at the wall, or better still, at an 18-inch circle drawn on the wall. You wouldn't ask me how to hold the ball, would you? You wouldn't ask me how to stand, either, but it may be wise to start out standing like this...

"With your right foot (if you are right-handed, or your left foot if you are left-handed) in line with the bullseye, stand comfortably, legs a little apart, at roughly a 45-degree angle to the toe-line. Now, put your weight a little onto your right foot, and lean gently toward the board, but lean from the leg, and not from the waist.

If your left foot starts to point down, that's perfectly OK. Looking at the board, your shoulder, waist, and foot should be pretty much in line with the middle of the board, and you are ready to throw.

"Don't even think about asking: 'What should I aim for?' because all you want to do is hit the board, hopefully point first. You have thrown your first dart, but you still have another two left, so throw them.

"Now for something that most complete beginners do not usually think about: you have to retrieve your own darts.

"Repeat this exercise, remembering to extend your arm in a full follow-through, and trying not to look—or feel—like you are scared of throwing the dart. Also, try to avoid bending your knees, bouncing, hopping, or lunging. Repeat for as long as you wish. You will undoubtedly

become more comfortable with what you are doing as time passes, and you will probably start making some minor adjustments to your stance and throw as a matter of course."

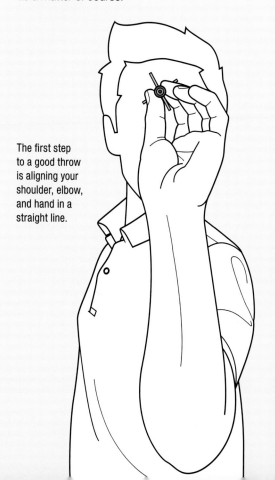

The first step to a good throw is aligning your shoulder, elbow, and hand in a straight line.

Practice

"Certainly in one's formative years, practice is vital, and the hours of pounding the board relentlessly can bring great reward. One thing to remember is that there are different modes of practice. The most obvious is a practice session to work on accuracy, but it is also a very useful tool for refining mechanics. I will say that the top players are constantly looking to make minute adjustments mechanically, in order to get that little extra out of their game."

GROUP THERAPY

"For newcomers to the game, by far the most important thing to work on is grouping; you will never get anywhere if you can't put three darts together on the board. The easiest way to do this is to throw your first dart at the board; wherever it lands (other than in the wall, an item of antique furniture, or worse still, the cat…) try to hit that dart with the other two. Keep doing that until you can consistently put the three darts somewhere close to each other. Then, you can start worrying about specific targets.

"One should practice hitting every segment on the board, as there will be a need to hit all of them at one time or another. The practice you have had with groupings should help, but then we move on to something a little more challenging—switching from one number to another during the throw. This is where a lot of players will struggle, and if you can become comfortable with this, it will help. For example, throw the first dart at the 20, the second at the 19, and the third at the 18. Try this with different combinations of numbers, even incorporating doubles and trebles.

"This leads into a more precise routine for players who play competitive darts. Sure, you need to practice doubles, but there is a lot more to it than that. Most experienced players are quite comfortable shooting at a finish of say, 81; it's not that difficult. It is also pretty easy to hit a treble 20, right? However, try putting those two shots together for a 141 finish, and it immediately becomes a whole lot more difficult. So, working on these combination shots is important.

Pro Tips

PRACTICE ALONE

"Personally, I find it easier to replicate match situations by practicing alone. That way, there are no outside distractions. What I will say is that for competitive darts, competition is by far the best practice you can get.

"That can help, but it's not always possible. So many players seemingly play to the level of their competition, and if that is the case, then that can be a major handicap. It doesn't matter how good or how bad your opponents are; they do not throw

Steve Brown, aged 15, poses with his late father, the darts player Ken Brown, in 1978.

your darts, and you do not throw theirs. The same as golf, bowling etc., the only thing that matters is what you do with your darts, and when you walk to that oche, the only thing that stops you from hitting what you are aiming at is *you*.

"Actually, to digress slightly, aiming in darts is done with the arm, and not with the eyes. It doesn't matter where you are looking if your arm doesn't follow suit. Remember, your darts will not always go where you aim them, but they will *always* go where you throw them..."

QUALITY CONTROL

"Sometimes practice isn't varied and interesting, but as long as one is single-minded enough to put in the time and effort, and can accept that it is necessary, that is not usually a problem. However, if you really don't feel like practicing, don't, and if your practice session isn't going well, quit. All that will happen in these situations is that you will become increasingly frustrated, which is the last thing you want. Bad practice is worse than no practice. Oh, and as time goes on, quality of practice will far outweigh quantity of practice."

Chapter Five: PLAYING THE GAME

Darts is a simple game with straightforward rules but that does not mean it is a sport without subtleties. This chapter covers all you need to know to get started, plus an introduction to some of the strategies that can help improve your game, such as the art of finishing and how to plan your approach to stay one step ahead of your opponent during the course of the game. In addition, Steve Brown dispenses more invaluable tips and tricks from his professional career.

Andy Hamilton
retrieves his
darts at the
2010 PDC World
Championship.
Andy is known for
his "aggressive"
style of gameplay.

Game On:
The Basics

Deciding who throws first is done either by the toss of a coin or by each player throwing a single dart at the bullseye, with the player whose dart lands closest being the one to throw first. The first player's dart should be left in the board unless it lands in the inner or outer bull, in which case it should be removed in order not to block the second throw. Player two can ask the referee to straighten the first dart if it is in another part of the board but obscuring the bullseye. If the two throws are equidistant from the bullseye, the procedure is repeated.

Each throw consists of three darts, thrown one at a time from a standing position from behind the toe-line. The thrower can rest their front foot against the back of a raised oche but placing it on or in front of any part of a raised or flat oche is not permitted. Players are allowed to throw from either side of the oche provided that they remain behind the back line.

A throw may only consist of fewer than three darts if a player checks out (finishes the game) with their first or second dart. Darts that are thrown by mistake after a player has checked out do not count.

The point of a dart must be touching the board for it to score. If any other part of the dart than the point is touching the board, the dart does not score. Also, if a dart misses the target area or bounces out, it does not score and cannot be thrown

again. An exception to this rule occurs in soft-tip darts, where a dart may register on the electronic scoring and bounce out and therefore counts as a scoring dart.

Darts only count after the referee or chalker has called the total score and the thrower has retrieved their darts from the board. If a dart is in danger of falling from the board a player may only cross the toe-line to secure it in the board, but only after they have thrown all three darts. Likewise, if a player drops a dart over the toe-line, the referee may allow them to retrieve it and throw it again.

A player may ask the referee or chalker to check their own or their opponent's score before they throw. However, the official is allowed to call the total score only and the player is not

The officials stand by the scoreboard at the 2010 PDC World Championship.

1980
Eric Bristow, the "Crafty Cockney," wins the first of five BDO World Championship titles in a seven-year spell in which he becomes indisputably the greatest player of his generation.

allowed to ask for advice on how to finish. For example, the referee may confirm that a player requires 36 but they must not tell them that they need double-18 to check out.

SCORING

Scoring is simple in darts. A dart landing in the 20 scores 20 points, unless it hits the outer or doubles ring, in which case the score is multiplied by two to 40 points, or the inner or trebles ring, which multiplies the score by three to 60, and so on for each number. The two segments of the bullseye are worth 25 points and 50 points for the outer and inner respectively.

The most commonly played darts game is 501, in which each player starts on that number of points and then subtracts the total scored with each throw, continuing until one player reaches zero and wins the game. However, to finish the game, or check out, as it is known, the player must usually throw a double. For example, a player with 18 points left must hit double-9, rather than a single 18, to check out. The inner bull counts as a double 25 for the purpose of finishing.

There are numerous other darts games, which are covered in depth in the chapter "Fun and Games,"

Scoring is relatively easy to master in comparison to finishing.

(page 124). Straight-scoring games such as 501 are the most popular, although the starting point can be any number: 301, 701, and 1001 are all common variations. In some games, players must start by throwing a double and darts only score once this has been done, while in soft-tip darts, players can sometimes finish on a single number.

The score is called by the referee and recorded by the marker or scorer, except in soft-tip darts where the machine records the score electronically. In competitions the scores should be displayed at eye level and for this purpose most dartboards in pubs and bars will have an adjacent chalkboard, which is why the scorer is often called the chalker. The scores should be set out so that each score and the remaining points for each scorer are clearly marked.

GOING BUST

As the name suggests, this is something to avoid at all costs. The bust rule means that a player must not score equal to or more than the number they require to finish, otherwise the darts will not count and their score will revert to the number it was prior to that throw. For example, if they need 48 to check out and they hit 16, 16, and 16 (the last instead of double 8) their score reverts to 48 and it becomes

Kevin Painter, "The Artist," at the 2010 PDC World Championship.

1984
John Lowe wins £102,000 for recording the first televised nine-dart 501 against Keith Deller in the BDO World Matchplay. For good measure, Lowe completes a rewarding week's work by winning the title for the only time in his career.

their opponent's turn to throw. In games that finish on a double, a player also busts if they score one fewer than the number they require, as it is not possible to finish on a double with one point left.

ETIQUETTE

Darts is rare among sports in that players never try to bend or break the rules. A game of honor, it has its own etiquette that players should follow at all times, whether they are professionals contesting a championship final or amateurs having a friendly game. Here are some dos and don'ts to ensure games are always played in the right spirit.

Do ensure that every game of darts begins and ends with a handshake with your opponent.

Don't stand in your opponent's eyeline when they are throwing. Instead, stand behind them.

Do play at a correct pace and not deliberately slowly or fast in order to disrupt the tempo of your opponent.

Don't distract your opponent when they are throwing by moving or making any kind of background noise.

Do congratulate your opponent when they have thrown well, but only do so after they have thrown all three darts.

Don't curse or react negatively no matter how well or badly you or your opponent throws.

Do ask the referee, scorer, or chalker what your score is if you are unsure, but don't ask what number you should aim for next. Only a teammate is allowed to proffer this advice.

Do remove your own darts from the board after each throw.

Don't throw a dart at the board in anger, for example if you have already bust with your first or second dart.

Above all, **do** remember to enjoy playing the game at all times.

SHARP PRACTICE

An exception to the unwritten rule that players should retrieve their own darts occurs in American darts, where the players share a set of darts whose sharp points make it safer for the player throwing next to take them from the board themselves.

In American darts, players share darts so that the next player can view and verify the score of the preceding player. It is also safer to remove sharpened darts yourself, grasping them away from the tips, than it is to be passed a handful of three darts.

Finishing

In darts, consistently high scoring is obviously a key facet of the game, but no less important is the ability to finish. Most -01 games must be finished on a double, and hitting these when it matters demands accuracy, of course, and a degree of nerve. But it also helps to be able to plan ahead and to think on one's feet; to know which numbers to hit as well as be able to hit them.

THINK AHEAD

At the start of a game of 501, the tactics are straightforward; a player needs to accumulate as many points as possible as quickly as possible. At this stage it is easy for the thrower to get into a good rhythm as they are aiming only for the higher numbers on the board.

But as the score remaining decreases, the tactics must change so that the player can work down to finishing on a double. As well as being the most crucial part of the game, finishing is arguably the most difficult, for a number of reasons: doubles are small targets; a player close to

victory can be affected by tension; and often players are uncertain of the best shot under the circumstances.

The first two of those factors will improve with practice and experience, but the third is often neglected, surprisingly so, since it can fast help a player's game. Therefore it's worth putting in a little time and effort in order to familiarize oneself with this aspect of darts.

Many recreational players will only start to think about what double to finish on when they get to a score they are confident of making in three good darts, perhaps between

50 and 100. Even those who play at a more competitive level underestimate the value of the set-up shots that lead to an easier finish. Many will score heavily on the 20 until they get below 200 and then think about the best way to check out. Instead, they should be planning their finish even earlier than that. The top professionals will start this process when they get to about 350, and a 180 will leave a 170 finish.

That is the highest score on which a player can check out and from that number downward, there are numerous combinations for how to finish (for example: a player requiring 140 could hit two treble 20s and a double 10; a treble 20, bullseye, and double 15; a treble 20, treble 16, and double 16—the permutations are many).

What is important to note here is that to finish well, a player will need to be adept at switching quickly between targets and counting down in their head to determine the next number to aim for. If they take too much time to stop, think, and recalculate between throws, then it will affect their rhythm and, in turn, their accuracy will suffer.

Mark Dudbridge quietly celebrates after winning a leg at the 2010 PDC World Championship.

SWEET 16s?

Some doubles are more advantageous than others. As a general rule, even-numbered doubles (double 16, double 8 etc.) are "friendlier" than odd-numbered ones (double 19, double 13 etc.) for one simple reason: if a player missed an even-numbered double on the inside and score a single of that number, they still leave themselves with a double. In the same situation with an odd-numbered double, they are left with an odd number and can't finish with their next dart.

A good tip for new players is to work their way down to 32, as it increases the chance of leaving "double-friendly" numbers such as 16, 8, and 4 if they miss on the inside. However, one should not become obsessed with this tactic: leaving double 20 is ideal if you are good at hitting it.

RECAP ON YOUR TACTICS

You	Your opponent	Your tactic
On a finish	On a finish	Go for it!
On a finish	Not on a finish	Go for it or work down to your favorite double
Not on a finish	Not on a finish	Work down to your favorite double or finish

Setting Up

"Imagine we're playing 501. If I start the leg, I will have three more darts to finish the leg than you; if you don't finish in 15 darts, I have three more. If you then fail to leave yourself on an out, or fail to give yourself a chance of setting up an out, you have given me three more darts. Do you really want to give your opponent a six-dart advantage?!

"You may think setting yourself up is too mathematical, but it really isn't; it's all memory. The example in this chapter with 126 is perfect: if you didn't know it already, you now know that 126 under pressure is 19s first (four 19s and a bullseye or two treble 19s and double 6). Remember that. If you can learn these outs, remember them, and become comfortable with them, you will give yourself a much greater chance of winning."

AN ADDED ADVANTAGE

It's an asset to be familiar with different scoring combinations—but the good news is, you don't have to be a mathematician.

There are thousands of combinations for outshots, but learning these is not just about knowing what any two or three numbers added together make. The more you play and the more you learn from your experiences, the more it will become apparent you can often play percentage shots. How you determine this depends on the match situation.

> ### 1986
> Englishman Bob Anderson, the "Limestone Cowboy" defeats Bob Sinnaeve, of Canada, to begin an unprecedented run of three successive victories in the Winmau World Masters.

Let's say you require 126 to finish. **If your opponent cannot finish**, it is advisable to do whatever is most comfortable and to try and leave yourself on your favorite double. This is because whatever your opponent does you are guaranteed another throw. **If your opponent is on ANY finishable number**, the situation is different and you should finish in three darts, because they may be your last three of the game. When you get to know your finishes, you will realize that the best approach is to aim for treble 19 first. A single 19 will then leave you a bullseye to finish. If you hit a single 19 instead of the treble, you still have two darts to go for treble 19 and bullseye and finish. Many players would aim for treble 20 first, as it's the highest score

on the board, but if they hit single 20, they cannot finish with their remaining darts.

THE IDEAL SET-UP

Top players start thinking about setting themselves up for their outshot from a very early stage. In a game of 501 this is usually around the 350 mark but it can be earlier.

Suppose, in a game of 501, that a player starts by throwing 100 with their first three darts, leaving them on 401. Their next two darts are single 20 and treble five, making the score 366. Now the temptation is to aim for the highest number again but if they miss and hit the singles, it will take at least three turns to finish from 346.

Instead, the percentage shot is to aim for the 19, because a single will leave 347 and that can be finished in two turns (180 and 167), and a treble will leave 309, which also can be finished in the next two turns.

On the next pages, Steve Brown has put together some of the set-up shots that could make a huge difference. They all assume that you are the player walking to the oche to throw next.

306

19s first. Single 19, treble 19, treble 20 leaves 170.

Treble 19, treble 19, and an outer bull leaves 167.

If you shoot the 20 first, and only hit a single, you cannot leave an out.

303

The same principle. Seven 19s will leave 170.

302

You can shoot 18s first, as a first dart single 20 won't get you to an out, but you may not always get full value from a treble.

Say you hit a treble 18 first dart, to leave 248. Stay on 18s, knowing that a single will give you a shot at the treble 20 with your third dart to leave 170. What happens if you hit another treble 18? Personally, I would stay on the 20, and then, if I hit the treble, I would switch to 18s.

269

So often I see players shoot two single 20s, and then realize that they cannot leave a finish. Take the 19s first; if you hit a single then four 20s will leave 170.

If you hit a treble 19 it will give you a shot at single 20 and outer bull to leave you 167.

268

I like four 19s and an outer bull to leave 167.

Even two single 19s will give a chance to leave 170 with a treble 20.

266

20 first, then four 19s to leave 170.

265

Five 19s will leave 170.

263

19 first, then four 20s to leave 164.

262

20 first, then four 18s to leave 170.

259

Same as 269 only to leave 154.

235

Two single 20s put you on 195, then an outer bull is the shot.

234

Single 19, outer bull, and single 20—three singles in a line up the board—leaves 170. A treble or inner bull is a bonus.

233

Two single 19s and an outer bull will leave 170.
Four 19s and an outer bull will leave 132.

232

Same as 235, except that you will leave 167.

231

Same as 234, except that you will leave 167.

Chapter Six:
PLAYING
COMPETITIVELY

Millions of people treat darts simply as a relaxing and enjoyable pastime, but millions more play the game at a more serious level, with an elite few going on to make a professional career from the game. This section of the book takes a look at competitive darts and the different approach that playing at a higher standard demands of a player. Steve Brown is on hand to offer more advice, including a fascinating exploration of the psychology of the game.

The crowd at the 2010 PDC World Championship celebrate James Wade's exciting victory against Andy Hamilton— Wade came within a dart of being knocked out by "The Hammer."

Gospel according to...
Phil Taylor

Perfection

"I have come close to the perfect match a few times. Probably the closest was against Gary Mawson at the 1997 World Matchplay in Blackpool. In the last three legs of the game I took out 501 in 11, 10, and 10 darts. I won the match 8–0 and Gary got down on his knees afterward.

Phil Taylor celebrates becoming the 2009 World Darts Champion at London's Alexandra Palace in 2009.

"That same year, one leg I can remember was when I was playing Martin Adams, the England captain, in the semi-final of the News of the World Championship. It was the best of three legs and he went 1–0 up. In the second I was way adrift but hit 177 [two treble 20s and a treble 19] and then took the leg on double 12. I went on to beat him 2–1 and did a little war dance for victory afterward.

"Then, in the final against Ian White, it was £42,000 [$70,000] for the winner and a set of gold darts. I went 1–0 up against the darts and, second leg, I kicked in with two 180s and thought: 'How's that then!' I'd got this far and wasn't going to lose. It was a title I was desperate to win. Unfortunately I didn't do a nine-darter but took the title by closing out the leg in 12 darts.

"Then there was that leg against James Wade in Blackpool in 2008 (in the World Matchplay final). He went 180, I went 180, he went 180, I went 180. He went treble 20 but then missed treble 19. I missed treble 20 on my seventh dart but went on to win the final 18–9."

Preparation

As the saying goes: if you fail to prepare, then prepare to fail. This is true at every level of competitive darts, from a local league match to a world championship final.

NO TIRED EXCUSES

Darts may not appear the most physically demanding of sports, but rest and physical preparation are both very important. In a pub team match a player might have relatively long spells between legs, while a professional may play the best of five sets, with five legs to each set, without a break. Adequate rest will ensure a player walks to the oche for their first throw relaxed and refreshed whatever the type of match.

It is also important to be prepared for the particular format being played. For short matches, a player needs enough recent practice to hit the ground running.

For longer matches, they must be confident that they have the stamina to keep throwing for a long period of time so they have to make sure that it is used to extended periods of play.

In the United States, round-robin play presents a challenge for the competitive player, as it requires them to play several short matches over a long period of time. In such instances it is vital to pace oneself. As opposed to a straight knockout, where victory means progress to the next round and defeat means a journey home, in the round-robin format a player can still be in contention after an early loss or losses. It's important to maintain an even keel.

DRESS SENSE

The world's best players do not just practice, practice, and practice again to reach the top. They also look at all the other facets of the game in which they can gain an advantage, however small, over their opponents. The top darts stars also ensure that they are properly attired.

There are strict rules governing what professionals may wear on the oche, where denim jeans are banned, for instance. Comfortable clothing is essential, and a short-sleeved shirt that does not restrict the throwing arm is a must. Shoes are also important in a game where a comfortable stance is vital and players may be on their feet all evening. Anything that is too tight or constricting is out; something with a good arch support, or at least good orthopedic insoles, is recommended.

GETTING IN THE ZONE

Top sportsmen often talk about being "in the zone," but time zones can also present a challenge, especially as the very best players now compete in all parts of the world.

Although this isn't an issue that is likely to trouble the league player, it's worth studying how the leading pros deal with it. A difference of one or two hours is not hard to handle, but traveling between the US and Europe can play havoc with the body clock. Players will fly in a few days early for a tournament, to enable the body to adjust at the accepted rate of one hour's time difference per day.

Simon Whitlock's unique forward-facing throwing action in the PDC World Darts Championship in London, 2010.

Sportsmanship

Emotions can run high during a game of darts, especially in a close match, and it is easy to feel disappointment, frustration, and even anger, as a result of a loss or a poor performance. That is perfectly acceptable.

However, it is important that a player never directs negative emotions at their opponent. Even at the top level, you will often see players acknowledging a big shot from their opponent, so there is no reason that it shouldn't be the same in local leagues and tournaments.

Likewise, the cheating (intentionally claiming that you've scored something you haven't), bad behavior and gamesmanship that are common in other professional sports are taboo.

Other actions that are frowned upon include:

• Heckling your opponent (talking, banging darts together, rattling loose change in your pocket, etc.) while they are throwing.
• Standing too close behind your opponent while he is throwing.
• Walking straight back up the middle of the oche after retrieving your darts.
• Running off to the bar—or the bathroom—during a match, and making everybody wait.
• Taking 10 or 15 minutes to get to the board after you have been called up for a match.
• Celebrating in your opponent's face.

And, at all levels of the game, from the professional ranks to the pub game, players must respect the match officials: the referee, caller, scorer, or chalker. Watch closely and you will see that all the best professionals greet the officials before a match and thank them afterward.

1988
Steve Brown, of "The Darts Bible" fame, completes the first of his back-to-back victories in the North American Open Darts Tournament, which attracts more than 2,000 players for the first time in its history.

DARTS AND COACHING

According to Steve Brown, who has contributed much of his expertise to this book, coaches are pretty much non-existent at present, although it is an area that has always interested him. "I do regard myself as something of one," Brown says. "It is not always a bad idea to have someone watching you when you practice, watching for things that you should —or shouldn't—be doing.

Setting up a camcorder is also a good idea. The main things to look for are a solid and comfortable stance, a smooth and positive stroke, and a full follow-through."

SETTING GOALS

All darts players dream of overnight success, but even the greatest of them all, Phil Taylor, had to work his way up through small tournaments before becoming a professional and going on to rule the world. So the trick with setting goals is to make them realistic and achievable, otherwise it is all too easy to lose confidence when they are not attained.

BEING A PROFESSIONAL

The ever-increasing financial rewards on offer in the game make professionalism an attractive option for the better players. But as with all other sports, the high-earners represent the tip of the iceberg and there are countless others beneath them who have discovered to their cost the ruthless nature of playing for a living.

As Steve Brown says: "Simply put, being a professional means that I have to rely on winning to put money in the bank; if I don't win, I don't get paid. That can add pressure sometimes, but players wouldn't be doing it for a living if they couldn't handle the pressure! What I will say is there are easier and financially better ways of making a living than playing darts, but personally, I couldn't think of anything better to do!"

Ted Hankey kisses the trophy after winning the BDO World Championship final against Tony O'Shea, 2009.

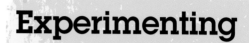

Gospel according to...

Phil Taylor

Experimenting

"I'll always try something different. I've tried different stances, different clothes, different shoes. Everything. If you tell me you've seen the perfect shoes for playing in, I'll go out and buy seven pairs. Then I might wear one pair on a Monday, another on Tuesday, Wednesday. It lets them recuperate;

Phil Taylor competes against Raymond van Barneveld during the Premier League, 2009.

it's millimeters, isn't it? If you wear a pair of shoes you'll squash them a little, wear them down. That sometimes can make a difference between playing well and not playing well.

"I shaved my hair off once and it created quite an interest in the press. It wasn't to improve or anything—I just needed to get my hair cut. But people thought I'd done it to improve my technique or stance or something.

"It's sort of psychological as it works and intimidates players a little more.

"I'm thinking: 'Don't concentrate on me, concentrate on your own game.' If you're concentrating on me, it's brilliant for me because you're not paying enough attention to your own game.

"I wonder sometimes how players in this sport and other sports never win anything but still do the same things. Over and over they prepare the same, practice the same, and I don't understand it. If somebody builds a wall and it isn't right and it's about to fall down they wouldn't do the same thing the next week. But some players keep doing the same things as a matter of routine."

Experimenting

Psychology

"It is often said that darts is 90 percent mental, but I do wonder if that's a conservative estimate!

"As far as I know, psychologists aren't particularly common in darts, although they could prove useful. The problem is that, while I can teach you to physically throw your dart, I can only advise you on what you need to do with your head—the rest is down to you. What I will say is that everybody gets nervous at times; we cannot usually prevent the onset of nerves, so all we can do is to learn to control them. However, that is something that comes with experience, so the more you put yourself in certain situations, the easier it should become.

"Usually, nerves and tension come as a result of negative thoughts, but it is often very difficult to prevent these thoughts from jumping out and messing with you; it's like we have a natural 'self-destruct' button in our heads! There are a number of different scenarios that are most likely to have you quaking in your boots, and I haven't sufficient space to cover them all here, but here is one of the most common...

"You are playing me, and you have 40 left. I'm back on 212. You are probably thinking, 'Cool, I've got this!' It's my shot, though, and I walk up there and hit a 180 to leave 32. Now what are you thinking? Probably, 'Oh, I've got to hit this now!' Why?

"Realistically, I have not changed your shot—or your chance to win—in any way. You still have the same three darts at it, and even if you do miss, there is no guarantee that I will finish. Trouble is, that's not the way you feel, and you miss, so, why do these negative thoughts hit us like that? Sorry, but I don't know the answer. All I know is that I don't usually allow myself to be put in that situation; I still focus on the positive aspect that my opponent has not been able to take the winning shot out of my hands.

"There are other situations that can be intimidating, such as playing in front of a crowd or playing on stage, and this is where another simple, but frequently devastating thought hits us: 'I really hope I don't embarrass myself!' If that's what you are thinking, then that's probably what is going to happen. Playing on stage is actually no different to playing down the pub. You are playing with the same darts, on the same board, from the same distance, yet most players make it different."

Dartitis

"It is amazing just how many people are still ignorant of this affliction, and it's disturbing to see victims ridiculed and abused when they are suffering. For those who don't know, dartitis is a physical inability to release the dart. Yes, it sounds strange, even laughable, but for the many players who have struggled with it over the years, it is anything but amusing.

"Despite much research, we still don't know exactly what it is, and why it happens. You may have seen articles claiming, 'This is why it happens' and 'This is how to cure it,' but if it was that easy, well...

"Different players are affected in different ways and, as a result, the remedies can be very different; what works for one may not work for

1990

Phil "The Power" Taylor, beats his mentor Eric Bristow to win the BDO World Championship for the first time and begin an extraordinary 20-year domination of the sport.

another. We know it's in the head, but it is not simply nerves or tension. It really can't be that easy, because as I said, we all get nervous, and still relatively few of us suffer from dartitis. It is far more sinister than that.

"Some are affected mainly on their first dart, and others on all three. Some are affected most of the time, others only at times of extreme pressure. Some lose all accuracy, while others—surprisingly enough—suffer little accuracy loss. It affects players of all different ages, temperaments, and skill levels.

"Some recover to the extent that you would never guess that they had once suffered, yet others never get over it. Many have ended up quitting the game they love because of it. All I will say is that anyone who suffers from dartitis has my sympathy, and they should have the sympathy of other players also. Don't you think they would throw the dart if they could?"

Probably the most famous player to have suffered from dartitis is Eric Bristow, the five-times world champion. Bristow developed the condition in 1987, a year after the last of his world title victories, but managed to make a recovery and, although he was never again the force of old, succeeded in regaining the world no. 1 ranking in 1990.

Chapter Seven: FUN AND GAMES

Straight-scoring darts games—such as 501 and 301—are the most commonly played, especially at the professional level. But darts is enjoyed by players of all standards and in all manner of ways, and this chapter looks at some of the most popular games that can be enjoyed by everyone from the complete beginner upward. In addition, there is also an in-depth look at the game of Cricket, with tips from Steve Brown on the strategies and tactics of the game. So if you never imagined that you might score a hole-in-one or bowl a perfect game with a dart, then read on…

In "Round the Clock" the last shot must be the bullseye.

Down to Zero

When darts was first played, the winner was the player who achieved the highest score with an agreed number of throws or was the first to reach a set target. However, over the years, something of an about-turn took place and darts is now almost unique among target games in that the scores are counted down from a pre-determined number to zero.

This is believed to have derived from the card game Cribbage, which was played in English alehouses from the eighteenth century and remains a popular pub game. To keep a record of the points scored in Cribbage each player inserted a peg in a crib board, which had two sets of 60 holes on each side plus one extra pegging-out hole at each end. The crib board became used for scoring in darts, with single games starting on 301—equal to five times around the crib board (5 x 60) plus one. The single extra point made darts a greater test of skill because players could not just stick to throwing at round numbers. Incidentally, when two players were on the same score and their pegs were next to

Above: Cribbage in action.

Right: The crib board.

each other, it gave rise to the phrase "level pegging" that is still used to describe tied scores in many sports.

In the nineteenth century, scores began to be kept on a chalkboard or blackboard but games ending in -01 numbers (101, 301, and 501) continued to be the most popular. When the world's first nationally organized darts tournament, the News of the World Championship, was inaugurated in 1927, it was decided that each game (or "leg") would be 501, and that remains the standard game at amateur and professional levels.

Above: Dominoes and cribbage being played in an old English tavern in the 1860s.

Straight Scoring

The shortest form of the game is played over a single leg between two players. To determine who has the advantage of throwing first, the players will either toss a coin or throw a single dart at the bullseye. The player whose dart is closest to the bull gains the honor of going first and is said to be throwing "with the darts." The second player, because they start at a disadvantage, is said to be throwing "against the darts."

In a single leg of 501, then, the score the first player achieves with their three darts is subtracted from the starting score and players then throw in turn, with the aim of being the first to reach zero. To make the game more challenging, players must generally finish (or "check out") with a double. So, for example, a player with 40 left will win if they hit double 20, or a 20 followed by a double 10. The inner bull counts as a double 25, so a player with 50 left can check out on an inner bull.

The requirement of finishing the game on a double means it is as important to be able to finish well as it is to score heavily; this can give a player who is well adrift on points a chance to catch up and win the game if their opponent is struggling to finish on a double. Occasionally, especially in soft-tip darts, games can finish on a single number, so a player needing 40 to check out can do so with two single 20s.

The minimum number of darts needed to win a game

of 501 is nine, and major professional tournaments often carry a significant extra cash prize for achieving this feat—the equivalent of a hole-in-one in golf, pitching a perfect innings in baseball, a 147 break in snooker, or a perfect game of 12 strikes in ten-pin bowling.

STRAIGHT SCORING: DOUBLE IN AND DOUBLE OUT

Straight scoring -01 games can be made more challenging by requiring players to throw a double before they start scoring. In such matches, the first double that is hit is the first dart that counts. Any double will suffice, including the bullseye (double 25), but it is obviously advantageous to start with a high-scoring one such as double 20.

The beauty of this format is that the advantage of throwing first can quickly disappear if the second player hits their starting double before the first player has done so; however, it is less suitable for less proficient players. One event that used the "double in" format is the North American Open, in which legs were also played over 301 rather than 501.

STRAIGHT SCORING: THE FREEZE RULE

In soft-tip darts, this rule exists as a handicapping mechanism in team play that reportedly was first introduced to prevent teams playing ringers (outside players of a much higher standard). It states that a player can only check out if their partner has a score that is equal to or lower than the combined scores of their opponents. If a player is frozen and gets to zero, they either go bust or lose the game, depending on which league or competition they are playing in.

STRAIGHT SCORING: SETS AND LEGS

In professional tournaments, longer matches are often contested over sets and legs. For example, a first-round match at the PDC World Championship is played over the best of five sets, the winner being the first player to reach three.

Each set comprises five legs (individual games) of 501 and the winner of the set is the first player to three legs, except in the final set, which must be won by two clear legs to prevent the player throwing first in the set having an unfair advantage.

As the PDC World Championship progresses,

Straight Scoring

Steve		Phil	
	501		501
100	401	60	441
45	356	100	341
26	330	60	281
180	150	41	240

sets remain the best of five legs, but matches become longer, increasing to the best of seven sets in the second and third rounds, nine in the quarter-finals, 11 in the semi-finals, and 13 in the final.

The advantage of throwing first alternates in each leg and each set. For example, player one will throw first in the first, third, and fifth legs of the opening set, player two in the second and fourth. In the second set, player two will throw first in legs one, three, and five, player one in legs two and four. This system evens out the advantage of throwing first. A player may therefore throw first in consecutive legs; for example, if they lose a set 3–1 throwing first in the fourth leg, it will still be their turn to throw first in the opening game of the next set.

Above: Straight scoring games can be made more challenging when players are required to throw a double before they can start scoring.

Other Games

ROUND THE CLOCK

This is one of the simplest games and an easy and enjoyable way to practice and improve. It can be played by any number of players, from one upward. Having decided in which order everyone will play, players throw three darts at a time, in turns, and the object is to be the first person to hit, in order, all the numbers on the board from 1 to 20, then the inner and outer bullseyes. Alternatively, players can agree to a set limit on the number of throws each, with the person who is on the highest number at the end of the game declared the winner.

• It is important to remember that numbers must be hit in order. So if player one throws and hits 1, 3, and 2 in that order, they must next hit the number 3 again.

• To make the game more challenging or for the purposes of practice, players can adapt the rules so that they score only on doubles or trebles.

• Another twist on the rules that can make Round the Clock more exciting is that if a player hits a treble they jump forward three numbers instead of one, but if they hit a double they drop back two numbers.

Round the Clock		
Steve	Phil	Stacy
2	2	-
3	3	3
3	3	3
5	5	5

Killer		
Steve	8	~~IIII~~
Phil	15	I
Trina	3	III
Stacy	7	~~IIII~~

KILLER

This is a great social game that is best played with four or more players. However, beware, it can reveal who your true friends are as the object is to be the last person standing.

Players' names are written down the left-hand side of the chalkboard and each throws a single dart at the dartboard *with their non-throwing hand*. The number they hit is allocated to them and written next to their name. If a dart misses the board or hits a number that is already allocated then the player must throw again until they hit their own number. At this stage, it does not matter whether the dart hits a single, double, or treble, only the number of the segment.

The players then revert to using the correct hand and, throwing in order, try to hit their own number five times, at which point they become a *killer*. A single counts as one hit, a double as two, and a treble as three; each hit is tallied beside the player's name and number on the chalkboard. Once a player has become a killer, they can target the numbers of other players, with each hit they score wiping out one, two, or three lives depending on whether they hit a single, double, or treble. The aim is to reduce each opponent to zero lives, at which point that player is out of the game. If a player drops below five lives, they stop being a killer and cannot target other players' numbers until they have restored their five lives. An alternative, quicker version of killer can be played by reducing the number of lives to three each.

MICKEY MOUSE

Also sometimes called Tactics, this is a game of skill and strategy for two players or teams.

The numbers and letters 20, 19, 18, 17, 16, 15, 14, 13, 12, T (for any treble), D (for any double), and B (for bullseyes) are written down the left-hand side of the chalkboard and the names of the teams or players across the top. Players must hit each number or category three times (trebles count for three hits, doubles for two, singles one) before they can score points on it. However, once their opponent has hit it three times as well, that number or category is closed and there is no further scoring on it. The winner is the player or team with the greater number of points once all the numbers or categories have been closed. If no points have been scored, the winner is the first to close all the numbers or categories.

The beauty of the game lies in deciding whether to rack up points or close down categories. Purists prefer to keep points-scoring low and make closing down the priority, but if a player is adrift on points, they may counter-attack and try to score heavily on numbers that are still open to get in front rather than close down categories. Likewise, a player who hits three treble

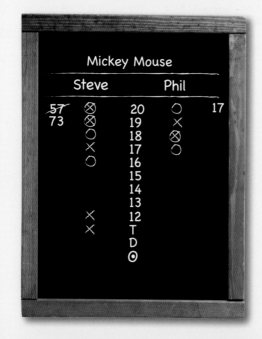

20s with their first throw may not choose to score any points but prefer to count it as three 20s and two trebles.

This game is one of the most popular soft-tip darts games, especially in the United States, where it is known as American Cricket but only the numbers 20, 19, 18, 17, 16, 15 and the outer and inner bullseyes are used. There are some quirky variations on American Cricket, including No-Score Cricket, in which no points are scored and the objective is solely to close down the numbers. Cut-Throat Cricket adds a nice twist in that a player or team's points awarded to their opponent(s) score and the winner is the player or team with fewer points.

Scram is American Cricket played over two rounds. In the first, player one tries to close down the numbers while player two scores points; in the second, the roles are reversed. The winner is the player who has the higher number of points after two rounds.

HALVE-IT

A "highest score wins" individual game that can be played by two people and upward but works best with groups of 6–12.

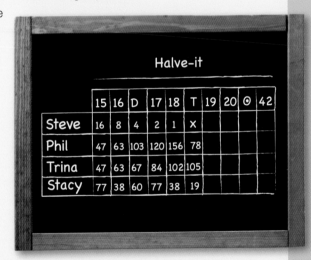

Halve-it

	15	16	D	17	18	T	19	20	Ⓞ	42
Steve	16	8	4	2	1	x				
Phil	47	63	103	120	156	78				
Trina	47	63	67	84	102	105				
Stacy	77	38	60	77	38	19				

The numbers and letters 15, 16, D (for any double), 17, 18, T (for any treble), 19, 20, B (for bullseyes), and 42 are written across the top of the chalkboard and the names of the players down the left-hand side. Players start with 32 points and, in turn, throw three darts at each number or category, starting with the 15 and working their way across round by round. The points they score are added to their total but if they fail to hit a required number or category, their score is halved. So, if a player hits a single 15 and a double 15 in the first round, 45 points are added to their 32, making 77. However, if they fail to hit a 16 in the next round, their score is cut to 39 (odd numbers are rounded up when halving). The winner is the player with most points at the end but if a player's score falls to 1 and they miss in the next round, they drop out of the game.

It is only possible to score on a number in its designated round, so if a player aims for 17 and hits a 15, the 15 does not count. In the final round, players must score exactly 42 with one, two, or three darts; a good tactic is to try to hit 16, 7, and 19, which are in the same area of the board and add up to 42. It is surprising how players come unstuck in this round. A feature of the game is that the greater the number of points a player has, the more they will lose if they miss a target, therefore it is more important to score in the later categories as the game can change dramatically toward the end.

There are many variations of this game. For instance, it can be played without the 32 points at the start (although this is a useful number for halving when less proficient players take part), without having to hit 42 at the end, or by nominating any categories or target you care to choose. It is also known by many other names, including 15–16… and double down.

NOUGHTS AND CROSSES OR TIC TAC TOE

For two players a noughts-and-crosses grid is drawn on the chalkboard and a different target is assigned to each section, with an inner bull in the middle square. The winner is the first player to hit a line of three targets either horizontally, vertically, or diagonally.

GOLF

For one or more players. The numbers 1 to 18 each represent the corresponding hole in a round of golf. The par for each hole is 4 and players throw one dart at each number, scoring par (4) if they hit a single of that number, a birdie (3) if they hit the treble, and an eagle (2) if they hit the double. However, if they miss the number or the board they score a bogey (5). An inner bull counts as a hole in one, but as a deterrent, the outer bull counts as a double-bogey (6).

Noughts + Crosses

T19	6	20
25	BULL	D16
5	T8	D1

Trina = ✕
Stacy = ◯

Golf

Hole	Steve	Phil
1	4	3
2	3	4
3	4	5
4	6	4
5	5	4
6	4	4
7	2	3
8	4	4
9	3	
TOTAL	35	

The winner is the player with the lowest 18-hole score at the end of the round and a tie can be settled by playing extra sudden-death "holes" on the 19 and 20 and, if necessary, back to 1 and onward again.

SHANGHAI

A simple game that can be played between any number of individuals or teams, Shanghai is a "highest score wins" game with a twist, which is that the highest score sometimes doesn't win.

Confused? To explain, the numbers 1 to 20 are written down the left-hand side of the chalkboard and, after throwing nearest the bull to decide the order of play, the names of the individual players or teams are written across the top. In each round, the object is to score as many points as possible on that number alone—so the 1 in round one, the 2 in round two, etc. The winner is the player or team with the highest points total after round 20 but at any time during the game, a player can Shanghai their opponent(s) and win the game by scoring a single, double, and treble on the particular number for that round. So if a player is 50 points adrift in round 15 but hits single 15, double 15, and treble 15 (in any order) they still win. However, the round must be completed to give everyone an

Shanghai				
	Phil + Steve		Trina + Stacy	
1	1	1	1	1
2	6	~~7~~	-	1
3	6	~~13~~	9	10
4	24	~~37~~	4	14
5	5	42	30	GAME
6				
7				
8				
9				
10				
11				
12				
13				
14				
15				
16				
17				
18				
19				
20				

equal chance and, if a player matches someone's Shanghai later in the round, the player or team with the highest number of points at that stage wins.

BASEBALL

A game for two players. The area covered by the numbers 9, 12, 5, 20, 1, 18, and 4 represents the diamond. As in baseball, players have nine innings, each consisting of three throws. A dart landing in a single-scoring section of any number on the field of play counts as a single, in any treble as a triple, and in any double as a double. A home run is scored by hitting the inner or outer bull but can only be attempted with the final dart of each innings. The maximum score per innings is three runs and the winner is the player with the highest score after nine innings. If the scores are level at the end, extra sudden-death innings may be played.

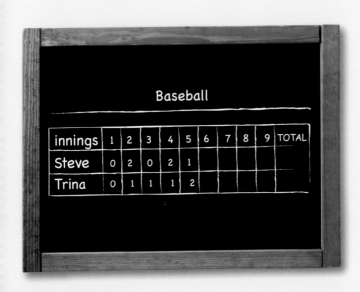

Baseball

innings	1	2	3	4	5	6	7	8	9	TOTAL
Steve	0	2	0	2	1					
Trina	0	1	1	1	2					

TEN-PIN BOWLING

For any number of players. Each throws two darts in each of 10 rounds, with the alley represented by the 20 segment. A treble equals 10 pins, a double 9, the outer single section 3, and the inner single section 7. A treble/ double combination earns a 2-point bonus and two treble 20s earns a 10-point bonus, so twenty consecutive trebles—admittedly a highly unlikely feat—constitutes the equivalent of a perfect game in bowling of 300.

OTHERWISE SCORING IS AS FOLLOWS:

Combination	Score
Two misses	0
Outer single and miss	3
Inner single and miss	7
Double and miss	9
Inner and outer single	10
Outer single and double	12
Inner single and double	16
Two doubles or double and treble	20 (includes two-point bonus)
Two trebles	30 (includes ten-point bonus)

As a variation, players can nominate a different number in each round.

FIFTY-ONE IN FIVES

For any number of players, this game of skill and strategy was originally played on Fives dartboards but is more challenging on a Clock board. Each player throws three darts per round and must make a score that is a multiple of five. All three darts must score for them to do so, and the total is then divided by five to determine the number of points they are awarded. For example, a score of 60 will earn 12 points. Any score that is not divisible by five is worth no points. The winner is the first player to reach exactly 51 points, meaning that a player on 45 points who throws 35 (which divided by five equals 7 points, taking their total to 52) goes bust and remains on 45 points.

SLIP-UP

For one or more players, this game is played on a Manchester log-end board but can be adapted for a Yorkshire board (without doubles) or a Clock board. Similar to Round the Clock, the objective is to get from 1 to 20 and finish on the bullseye, but there are some subtle differences. If a player hits a double they jump to the next number after that value. For example, if they hit double 1 with their first dart they move to 3, or if they hit double 9 they move to 19. Also, a player must hit the first double they hit again before hitting the bullseye. If they have not hit a double in reaching 20, they must hit double 1 before they go for the bullseye. The lowest number of shots in which it is possible to finish a game is seven: double 1, 3, double 4, 9, double 10, double 1 again, and the bullseye. If played on a Clock board, it is easiest to count darts that land in the treble as a single.

Cricket

THE BASICS

As mentioned earlier in the chapter, Cricket, which is also known as American Cricket, is a game in which two players or teams compete to own or close specified numbers on the board while also achieving a higher points score than their opponent or opponents.

The numbers used are 20, 19, 18, 17, 16, 15, and the inner and outer bullseyes. Each player or team takes turns to throw and in order to own a number (or inning, as it may be called in the US) must score three of that number, which can be done with three singles, a treble, or a double and two singles. For the purpose of scoring on the bullseye an inner counts as two bulls and an outer as one.

Once a number is in their ownership, they can score points on it until the opposition close it by scoring three of that number as well. The winner is the player or team that closes all the numbers first and has the most points, or, if both sides are tied on points, or have no points, the first player or team to close all the numbers. If a player or team closes all the numbers while behind on points, they must continue to score on any open numbers until they are in front in order to win.

Cricket is probably the most strategic darts game there is, and is enormously popular in the United States. As opposed to -01 games, where the tactic is always to score and finish quickly, in Cricket players can vary their tactics greatly, perhaps by choosing to close all the numbers, or to score points, or a mixture of both depending on the game situation. Although it may appear to be a complex game, it is simple to play.

Steve Brown's
Pro Tips

"Where a lot of players go wrong is that they don't know when to point, and when to close. Part of the reason is that they are not actually sure of the overall state of that particular leg of darts. I often ask players, 'When are you ahead in Cricket?' Points on the board is a pretty popular response. However, if you're playing me, and you have 20s and 100 points, yet I have every other number closed, do you still think that you're leading?

"The way that I gauge my position in the game is not by closed numbers or points, but by marks and by darts. Take the example I've just mentioned—extreme as it may seem. You are 100 points ahead, but what does that mean? I am not necessarily going to win the game as quickly as I suggest, but I can win the game in three darts; two treble 19s (to get the lead, pointwise) and a treble 20 to close. Therefore, I am theoretically just three darts away from the win."

IT ISN'T SO RUDE TO POINT

A significant difference between Cricket and similar games such as Mickey Mouse or Tactics is that Cricket, especially in the US, is often played far more aggressively and it pays to think two or three moves ahead, a little bit like chess.

Traditionally, deliberately scoring points on an opponent used to be frowned upon; the unwritten rule was that you should "only point if you're pointed" and the object was to close the numbers down quickly. But as the game has grown, it has also become more competitive and there are now many major Cricket tournaments, so that philosophy has changed and been replaced by a "win at all costs" approach, which means that it is not unusual to see 1,500 to 2,000-point legs.

Cricket

143

STARTING OUT

In straight-scoring games such as 301 or 501, there is a significant advantage to throwing first, because the relatively low number of points required to finish a game makes it difficult for the player throwing second to get far enough ahead to dictate the game. Another significant factor is that the winning shot is always in the hands of your opponent.

It might appear that the same is true in Cricket; that the player throwing first, if they are good enough, can simply force their opponent to play catch-up. However, the player throwing second can employ different tactics to prolong the game and, more importantly, take the winning shot out of the hands of their opponent.

TAKE CONTROL FROM THE OUTSET

One thing that is true regardless of whether a player throws first or second is that it is easier to win the game from in front. As mentioned earlier, this is difficult to do in -01 games but much more manageable in Cricket. The best plan is to dictate the game, to more or less force your opponent to shoot what you want them to shoot, or at least, stop them from doing what they want.

The way to achieve this is to be aggressive from the very start. But how? Traditionally, the best start in Cricket was considered to be treble 20, treble 19, treble 18, which gives the thrower ownership of three numbers. But although that is an excellent start, it can be matched by the second player, which would take the game back to square one.

Instead, a player hitting treble 20 with their first dart

could aim for two more treble 20s, enabling them to close the 20 and score 120 points. Now that can't be matched by player two.

It is always important to think what your opponent's strategy may be. Another good first throw would be two treble 20s and then a shot at treble 18, because player two may decide that, for them to dictate the game they should then start on 19 to own a number and score some points, but even if they hit seven 19s (two trebles and a single) it is easy for player one to regain the point lead because he can attack the 20 and 18.

A third good option, if a player hits treble 20 with their first dart, is to try to close the bulls with darts two and three. If the second dart hits the inner bull, the third can also be aimed at the bull. If the second dart is a single bull, the option is there to return to the 20 and point. Already, the first player has a foundation for owning the highest-scoring treble and the highest-scoring single.

KEEP YOUR NOSE IN FRONT

Because the most marks (single scores) a player can achieve with three darts is nine, a good yardstick in Cricket is to try and stay 10 marks ahead of the opposition. If that can be achieved, then even a perfect throw from them will not erase one's advantage. This is where it is possible to take the winning shot out of the hands of the opposition, even when not in a winning position.

It is perhaps best illustrated with an example:
Player One has 20s and 18s.
Player Two has bulls (Player One has none), two marks on the 20, and two marks on the 18. Everything else is dead.
Player One is 48 points ahead.

More often than not, **Player One** would be tempted to go straight for the bull, as they have a shot to win the game. That's fine, especially if they hit the inner bull first dart, but what if they hit the single, or worse still, miss with the first dart completely? Now, the pressure is really on. If they don't close the bull, they are leaving **Player Two** a very makeable shot.

An alternative approach would be for **Player One** to shoot the 20 first for points. A treble would leave **Player Two** 108 points down (five bulls), and even a single will leave them 68 points down. Even if **Player One** doesn't close the bulls, **Player Two** needs three bulls, single 20, and single 18, which they cannot hit in one turn.

After that, **Player One** could try the bulls, knowing that whatever **Player Two** does, they will have at least one more shot. If **Player One** hits the double or single bull, they should stay there. If they miss the bull with their second dart, another single 20 will put them 88 points ahead, and **Player Two** would now need four bulls, single 20, and single 18.

WASTED DARTS

Cricket players often talk of "wasted darts." What this means is that often a player will not get the full value of a treble or double because they already have a mark or marks on that number.

Here is an example that explains their importance: **Player One** starts the leg, and hits five 20s, choosing to own the 20 and score 40 points. **Player Two** responds with five 19s, choosing to own the 19 and score 38 points. If **Player One** hits single 19, single 19, treble 19, they can close the 19s but effectively they only score a single for that last-dart treble. If **Player**

Two then hits single 18, treble 18, treble 20, they can close 18s and take the points lead. A seven-mark shot has given them control of the game. Instead, if **Player One** hits single 18, single 18, treble 18, they now have 20s, 18s, and 76 points, earning full value for the treble and putting them in a better position than if they had targeted 19s. **Player Two** now needs nine marks (treble 19, treble 20, treble 18) to take control of the game. By changing the shot the same number of marks has put **Player One** in a much stronger position.

Dave vs *Chris*
—01 CRICKET —01

	20	X
	19	
	18	
	17	
	16	

Dave vs *Chris*
—01 CRICKET —01

80	⊗	20	X
		19	⊗
		18	
		17	
		16	

Dave vs *Chris*
—01 CRICKET —01

80	⊗	20	X	133
		19	⊗	
		18		
		17		
		16		

Dave vs *Chris*
—01 CRICKET —01

80	⊗	20	X	133
	○	19	⊗	
	○	18	○	
	○	17	○	
	○	16	○	

Chapter Eight: PROFESSIONAL PRIDE

Darts started out as a pastime and, for the vast majority of the millions of players worldwide, is still enjoyed as such. But from the 1960s onward, the growth of the game led inevitably to the advent of professionalism and the rise of players who would become famous the world over for their exploits on the oche. The story of how the working man's game became a world-class sport is a fascinating tale full of intrigue and larger-than-life characters.

T. P. Fox, winner of the News Of The World Individual Darts Championship, is presented with the trophy in 1937.

Working Class to World Class

Darts was played for the best part of a century before the advent of professionalism although, of course, games had always been played for money in the form of side bets.

In Britain, where the game first flourished in the first half of the twentieth century, regional events dominated the scene until 1938–39, when the *People* newspaper sponsored the first nationwide competition, the National Teams Championship. The timing was unfortunate, as the outbreak of World War Two in September 1939 meant that it was not played again until 1946–47.

The following year, the News of the World Championship, which had been played as a regional competition since 1927–28, became a nationwide tournament and Harry Leadbetter's victory made him the sport's first national champion. The News of the World event became the biggest prize in the game and, more significantly, in 1970 became one of the first events to be televised.

Although darts had first been shown on British television eight years before that, it was the screening of the News of the World Championship that fired the viewing public's attention and persuaded TV executives and sponsors that the game had a future on the small screen, helping to pave the way for the professional game.

By the end of the 1970s, the British Darts Organisation and the World Darts

Federation had both been formed, and the BDO had staged the inaugural World Professional Championship.

In the United States, where American-style darts—a game using extremely light wooden darts and a different board—had been played in Pennsylvania and its surrounding states since the late nineteenth century, the traditional game had been imported by British and Irish immigrants, as well as servicemen returning from duty in Britain during World War Two.

Here too, there was an explosion of interest in the game at the same time as the British game, with the US Open beginning in 1969, the North American Open starting the following year, and the American Darts Organization being formed in 1976.

Although a slight bust followed the boom of the 1970s, particularly in Britain where the interest of the TV companies waned, the formation of the Professional Darts Corporation in 1992 and the arrival of satellite broadcasting enabled the professional game to go from strength to strength.

By 2009, the total prize money for the PDC's five ranking tournaments had risen to $3 million (£1.8 million) and there were 70 countries under the umbrella of the World Darts Federation. No one could now question that darts had become a genuinely global, professional game.

The Entertainers

One of the first stars of the professional era, Alan Evans, has an unusual defeat on his career record. In July 1977, the Welshman played Muhammad Ali, the three-times World Heavyweight Champion (of boxing) in an exhibition match. Evans was allowed to score only on trebles and Ali won, finishing on a bullseye, and, not for the first time in his career, proclaimed himself "The Greatest."

A man playing darts at a nightclub in New York, 1943.

Darts on the World Stage

If any organization reflects the growth of darts in recent years, it is the World Darts Federation, membership of which is open to the game's official national body in all nations.

The WDF was formed in London in March 1976, with 15 founder members: Australia, Belgium, Bermuda, Canada, Denmark, England, Gibraltar, Ireland, Malta, New Zealand, Scotland, South Africa, Sweden, the United States, and Wales.

By the end of 2009, there were 70 countries affiliated to the WDF, as widely spread as Barbados, Botswana, Brazil, and Brunei. The remit of the Federation is to safeguard the status of its member bodies as representatives of their countries and to encourage the promotion of the sport of darts. It has more than 350,000 active playing members and sanctions in excess of 10,000 events worldwide.

The United States and the Netherlands have the largest memberships, with 50,000-plus playing members, while England has more than 20,000 active playing members, and Australia, Canada, and Germany more than 10,000 each.

The WDF organizes the World Cup—the premier event for national senior and youth teams, which has been played every second year since 1977—plus the Europe Cup, the Americas Cup, and the Asia-Pacific Cup. Results at the 2009 World Cup underlined the strength of the game, players from Holland, the United States, England, Finland, Australia, and Wales all winning titles.

Roy Price, the WDF president, believes that the appeal of the game will continue to spread: "In Europe, darts is taking off in the former Communist Bloc in places such as Poland, Serbia, Latvia, Estonia, Slovenia, and Lithuania," he explained.

"Darts is popular in Japan, where there are three different organizations, one of which, the Japan Sports Federation of Darts, is affiliated to the WDF. The game in the Far East and Asia appears to be stable. Malaysia, the Philippines, and Singapore are all affiliated to us.

"We do not know much about darts in China, although we know that darts is very popular in Shanghai and other major coastal cities in China and we have already initiated contact with the sports department of the Chinese government in Beijing." (Manufacturers of soft-tip equipment, some of whom base their production in China, say the game is growing fast there.)

But, says Price, the World Cup remains the WDF's greatest competition: "Most countries regard it as the highest honor still to represent their country at a World Cup. Things are slightly different in the United Kingdom and the Netherlands, in that the players are committed to the Professional Darts Corporation. But, otherwise, elsewhere in the world it's a great honor to play for your country, which makes the World Cup such a prestigious event."

1993

John Lowe becomes the first player to win the World Championship in three different decades in a tournament that turns out to be the last contested by players affiliated to both the British Darts Organisation and its new rival, the World Darts Council.

Fact:
In January 1990, Paul Lim threw the first nine-dart 501 in World Championship history. He achieved the feat in his second-round match against Jack McKenna of Ireland, hitting consecutive 180s before finishing treble 20, treble 19, double 12 to win £52,000 (approx. $77,000) in prize-money. It remained the only nine-dart finish in either the BDO or PDC World Championship until Raymond van Barneveld matched Lim in January 2009.

THE MAIN WDF EVENTS

World Cup

The flagship event of the World Darts Federation, held every two years since 1977.

Asia-Pacific Cup/Europe Cup/Americas Cup

Top international tournaments for each continent.

Dutch Grand Masters

One of the four WDF majors, with the BDO World Championship, Winmau World Masters and World Cup singles.

Star Turns

Mareno Michels, Joey ten Berge, Anthony Fleet, Steve Brown.

Joey ten Berge at the 2009 World Darts Championship.

The British Association

As the popularity of darts grew rapidly in Britain in the first half of the twentieth century, a number of leagues and competitions were introduced, mostly by breweries because the game was played mainly in local pubs.

With a variety of boards being employed in different regions, the need for a governing body soon became clear and the National Darts Association was formed in 1924, one of its first decisions being to adopt the Clock-pattern dartboard as standard.

The association did not survive World War Two, and in 1954 the National Darts Association of Great Britain (NDAGB) was founded to represent amateur players and organize their competitions.

Seven years later, Olly Croft threw his first dart at the Harringay Arms pub, in North London, little knowing the significant role he would come to play in the story of the game.

At the time Croft owned a family tile-fixing business, and he began to play darts to relax and unwind after work. He quickly became adept at the game and got involved in running inter-county competitions for the NDAGB and also formed the London representative side.

But arguably the most significant moment in the game's history came on January 7, 1973, when Croft met with other leading figures in the game to form the British Darts Organisation. Within one year, the World Masters had been introduced and within five, the World Championship was part of a BDO calendar that now encompasses 800 annual tournaments at all levels of the game.

"It didn't really happen overnight," says Croft. "There were two years of meetings before the BDO was formed. We wanted a body to be recognized both nationally and internationally for its professionalism and attention to the sport of darts."

The inaugural World Masters in 1974 featured 22 players, 10 from outside the British Isles, although it was an Englishman, Cliff Inglis, who prevailed. As Croft says, "I had made plenty of contacts around the world by that time and we felt that there was a real desire for that world event." He has been proved right by the success of the Masters, the 2009 version of which attracted players of both sexes from 70 countries, and the BDO World Championship which, despite the formation of the breakaway Professional Darts Corporation in 1992, remains a major event.

Croft was rewarded for his services to the sport in 2004 by being appointed OBE in the Queen's Birthday Honours List. "I was proud because it gave darts the recognition it deserved and recognized the people who had put so much into it," he recalls. "Now our long-term aim is to be part of the Olympic Games. We didn't make it for London 2012, and I don't know whether it will happen in my time, but we won't stop trying."

1994
Canadian John Part becomes the first North American player to be crowned BDO World Champion, while Englishman Dennis Priestley wins the inaugural PDC World Championship.

THE MAIN BDO EVENTS

BDO World Championship
Held annually at Lakeside Country Club, Frimley Green, Surrey.

Winmau World Masters Sport's oldest "major" dating back to 1974.

British Open
One of the sport's longest-running competitions, first played in 1975.

Inter-Counties Championship
Contested annually by 66 English, Scottish, and Welsh counties.

Star Turns
Ted Hankey, Martin Adams, Tony O'Shea, Trina Gulliver.

1995
Stacy Bromberg, of the United States, wins the North American Open Darts Tournament to begin a run of six successive victories that only ends after the event finishes in 2000.

Ribbons adorn the BDO World Darts Championship trophy, 2009.

Straight to the Heart

Rock City is now the premier music venue in Nottingham, England, but it began life as a bakery and, for a time, was a cabaret venue called the Heart of the Midlands Nightclub. It was under the last of these identities that it also earned a permanent place in the history of darts.

The Heart of the Midlands was the venue for the inaugural World Professional Championship in February 1978. Olly Croft, the founder of the British Darts Organisation, admits the inception of the tournament owed as much to the television companies as to the foresight of the BDO.

"As more players began to make darts their profession, there was a call for another major tournament," explains Croft. "The BBC [British Broadcasting Corporation] had seen the success of the World Masters on a rival broadcaster and wanted a piece of the action.

"The BBC were testing split-screen television at the time, so we got them on board early on. The split screen showing a closeup of the board and the player at the same time was a revelation."

Lasting five nights, the tournament brought international drama to the small screen. Sixteen players from eight countries took part. American Conrad Daniels thrashed England's Eric Bristow, the top seed and favorite in the first round, and a Welshman, Leighton Rees, won the title.

The World Championship immediately established

Darts commentator Sid Waddell at the 2008 PDC World Darts Championship in Alexandra Palace, London.

Fact:
Eric Bristow, the five-times world champion, was without doubt the first showman of professional darts. "The Crafty Cockney" was the best player of his generation, a fact he was never slow to let people know. After one win at the World Championship, he told a TV interviewer: "No one in the world can beat me, kid. You ask 'em all." Bristow had a distinctive style, with the little finger on his throwing hand raised, that he admitted toward the end of his career had been done "for show."

itself as an annual favorite and made famous not just the leading players, but also one of its commentators, Sid Waddell, whose excitable and colorful delivery have made him known the world over in his near-40 years at the microphone.

Waddell remembers the early years of the BDO World Championship as an exciting period for darts. "The first world final drew in four million viewers in Britain," he explains, "and within five years 8.3 million [15 percent of the population] watched the amazing Eric Bristow–Keith Deller final."

Since 1985, the championship has been played at the Lakeside Country Club in Frimley Green, Surrey, and despite the split that saw its leading players leave the BDO to form the World Darts Council (now the Professional Darts Corporation) in 1992, it has continued to thrive alongside the PDC World Championship since 1995. The BDO added a women's World Championship in 2001 and a global TV audience of more than 100 million now watches the event each year.

The Great Divide

After the professional game had enjoyed an early boom, there followed a downturn in fortunes in the late 1980s that left the BDO World Championship as the only televised event in Britain.

The continued lack of exposure led, in 1992, to 16 of the world's top players forming a breakaway group, called the World Darts Council, having been told by the BDO that the organization could not guarantee more TV coverage or more prize money.

The move heralded a legal battle between the two bodies, and the 1993 World Championship was the last in which BDO and WDC-affiliated players competed alongside each other.

Although the new organization began its own World Championship in 1994, it was not until 1997 that the dispute was settled and the WDC dropped its claim to be a governing body, changed its name to the Professional Darts Corporation and accepted the BDO and World Darts Federation as the game's ruling bodies for the UK and the world respectively.

The BDO, along with other affiliated national organizations such as the American Darts Organization, then chose to ban the 16 from all their tournaments after the group wore the WDC insignia at the 1993 World Professional Darts Championship.

However, the PDC has flourished since then, with events such as the Premier League and World Championship attracting huge attendances and large television audiences. Prize money has also rocketed; for example the total fund for the 2010 PDC World Championship was £996,000 (just under $1.5 million).

"It took the great split, led by players like Eric Bristow and Phil Taylor, to shake things up," said Sid Waddell, the television commentator. "Now it's just about the greatest show on Earth. The TV coverage is amazingly hi-tech, with cameras everywhere, and in some venues we have over 10,000 people, basically looking at the backs of a couple of players' heads."

Barry Hearn, the chairman of the PDC, believes the sport still has untapped potential. "At the start of my chairmanship I had a saying that I could smell money in the room and so it has proved," he said. 'But more importantly, the image of the way the game is perceived around the world has also improved."

The PDC runs events in Europe, the United States, and South Africa but is looking farther afield. "There are a few areas we can improve in," added Hearn. "Darts in America can improve and we're thinking of moving into the emerging Asian, Middle Eastern, and African markets." And in October 2009 it became apparent that Hearn had also been looking closer to home when he made a takeover bid for the BDO that was rejected out of hand by Olly Croft's organization.

The crowd at the 2010 PDC World Championship.

THE MAIN PDC EVENTS

PDC World Championship
Held annually at Alexandra Palace in North London.

UK Open
Features 168 players in an open knockout with no seedings.

Las Vegas Desert Classic
Replaced the North American Open on the darts calendar.

World Matchplay
Played over sets, rather than legs, at the Winter Gardens, Blackpool.

World Grand Prix
Now played in Dublin, Ireland, the Grand Prix replaced the World Pairs.

US Open
A relatively new tournament, started in 2007 when Phil Taylor won the inaugural title.

Premier League
Contested by top six players in the world rankings, plus two wildcards.

Star Turns
Phil Taylor, Raymond van Barneveld, James Wade, Anastasia Dobromyslova.

Alexandra Palace, London

1998
Raymond van Barneveld, of the Netherlands, becomes only the second non-British World Champion when he beats Richie Burnett, of Wales. Van Barneveld's victory avenges his defeat by the same player in the 1995 BDO World Championship final.

Fact:
Three-times world champion John Lowe (left) became the first man to throw a televised nine-dart 501 in his World Matchplay quarter-final against Keith Deller in October 1984. The Englishman hit two maximums before finishing treble 17, treble 18, double 18, and he earned £102,000 (approx. $152,000) for his feat. In contrast, when the American Dave Kelly threw the first perfect six-dart 301 in an American Darts Organization-sanctioned event, the 1981 L & A Open, starting and finishing on a double for good measure, his reward was a free Coca-Cola and a mention in a magazine.

Chapter Nine:
DARTS
SUPERSTARS

Since the professional game came into existence, darts has produced more than its fair share of superstars: men—and more recently, women—who have ruled the world with their stunning play. This chapter presents profiles of the ten greatest players in the history of the game, the leading ladies of the sport, and the rising stars to watch out for in years to come.

Darts on the world stage—the 2010 PDC World Championship.

Leighton Rees

Born: January 17, 1940 in Ynysybwl, South Wales

Died: June 8, 2003 in Ynysybwl, South Wales

Major victories: BDO world champion 1978, WDF World Cup (team and singles) 1977

A larger-than-life Welshman, with an effortless throwing action, Rees became the game's first World Champion in 1978 and did much to popularize darts during that period.

Rees was working in the storeroom of a motor spares company when he found widespread fame in 1974 by winning one of first televised darts competitions on *The Indoor League*, a British program that showcased pub games. He regained that title in 1976 and later that year became one of the first players to turn professional.

In 1977 Rees was a member of the Wales team that triumphed in the inaugural World Darts Federation World Cup, at which he also won the men's singles championship. He represented his country 77 times.

His greatest achievement came in 1978 when he was crowned World Champion, beating John Lowe in the final. Rees had earlier recorded the first televised 10-dart 501 during a thrilling quarter-final victory over compatriot Alan Evans. Nick Evans, the producer of BBC Television's coverage of that first BDO World Championship, said that the latter match was the one that first fired the viewing public's appetite for the game.

Lowe took his revenge on Rees in the following year's final, but although Rees reached only one quarter-final before he last appeared in the championship in 1990, he remained one of the most popular players on the circuit.

In 1980 he married his wife Debbie, a leading American darts player whom he met while playing in the United States. In later life he suffered from ill health and he died from a heart attack on June 8, 2003. A street in his home village is named in his honor—Leighton Rees Close.

Although he peaked at a time before big money entered the game, Rees had no regrets about his career: "The main thing is I have memories of a great era playing alongside the likes of Alan Evans, Eric Bristow, Bobby George, Cliff Lazarenko, and Jocky Wilson. Good times and great memories," he once said.

2000
Ted "The Count" Hankey completes a 6–0 whitewash of fellow Englishman Ronnie Baxter in the shortest BDO final in the competition's history, a 46-minute shootout that Hankey finishes with the highest possible checkout of 170 in the last leg.

Fact:
On December 18, 1976, Rees finished a game of 3,001 in 141 darts—scoring on only the bullseye—hitting 34 inner and 52 outer bulls.

John Thomas "Jocky" Wilson

The mercurial and hugely popular Scotsman was one of the game's leading players throughout the 1980s and won world titles at either end of the decade.

What made this achievement remarkable was that Wilson's technique was one of the most unusual the sport has ever seen. His whole body would move with every throw and this would be further exaggerated when he was under pressure toward the end of matches.

Wilson had worked as a coal delivery man and a miner before victory in a darts competition at a holiday camp encouraged him to take up the game professionally in 1979.

Eric Bristow and John Lowe were the two best players in the world at the time but

Born: March 22, 1950, in Kirkcaldy, Fife, Scotland

Major victories: BDO world champion 1982, 1989

Wilson soon emerged as a serious contender and went on to beat both in World Championship finals.

The first of these successes came in 1982, when Wilson, who had reached the last eight in each of the previous three years, followed up his achievement in finishing second at the Winmau World Masters by defeating Lowe 6–4 in a memorable final to be crowned champion.

He reached three more semi-finals and three quarter-finals in the next six years, before claiming a second world title in 1989, taking the scalp of Bristow 6–4 in a dramatic final that he had led by five sets to nil, and preserving his 100 percent record in the showpiece game.

Wilson was one of the 16 players who broke away from the British Darts Organisation to form the Professional Darts Corporation in 1993, but he drifted away from the game after his final televised appearance at the 1995 World Matchplay and the onset of diabetes to become a reclusive figure.

"I'm all washed up and finished with darts," he admitted at the time. "But I don't want anyone feeling sorry for me."

However, his name remains synonymous with the game and a measure of the esteem he is held in came in August 2009, when the PDC announced plans for the Jocky Wilson Cup, an annual competition between England and Scotland, with a format similar to that used in Davis Cup tennis, to be played annually from December 2009.

2001
Trina Gulliver, of England, becomes the inaugural BDO women's World Champion and embarks on a run of seven consecutive victories in the championship.

John Lowe

Born: July 21, 1945, in New Tupton, Derbyshire, England

Major victories: BDO world champion 1979, 1987, 1993
World Masters 1976, 1980
News of the World Championship 1981
WDF World Cup Singles 1981, 1991
WDF World Cup Pairs 1977, 1979, 1983, 1985, 1987, 1989
WDF World Cup Team 1979, 1981, 1983, 1987, 1991

Despite spending the peak years of his career in the shadow of the legendary Eric Bristow, Lowe holds a unique place in the game as the only man to win world titles in three different decades, and is arguably the most respected player in the game's history.

The Englishman is admired as much for his great sportsmanship as a fluid technique that many experts and commentators have described as the perfect throwing action.

Lowe's rivalry with his great friend Bristow was a dominant feature of the professional game in its early years. The two met on six occasions in the BDO World Championship with Lowe coming out on top just once, when he triumphed in the 1987 final.

Overall, Lowe lost six of the nine major finals in which he and Bristow met, but as a team they were almost unstoppable, winning six pairs titles together at the WDF World Cup. Lowe made more than 100 appearances for his country in a decorated international career.

He also appeared in the televised stages of the BDO and PDC World Championships for a record 27 consecutive years from the first championship in 1978 to 2004. His failure to qualify in 2005 came in his 30th year in the professional ranks.

Apart from winning the BDO World Championship in 1979, 1983, and 1993, Lowe's most notable feat was to become the first man to complete a televised nine-dart 501, against Keith Deller in the World Matchplay in October 1984.

Equivalent to a hole-in-one in golf or a perfect game in bowling, the feat earned the Englishman a £102,000 (approx. $152,000) prize—still the greatest reward for such a feat. "It was a huge thing to do. No one else had ever achieved it and everyone remembers the first," Lowe says. "Players today score more consistently, but they are not a lot better than Eric [Bristow] and I were back then."

2003
After winning eight consecutive PDC World Championship titles, taking—his career total to 10—Phil Taylor is defeated in the final by John Part, who joins Dennis Priestley and Taylor as the only men to win both versions of the world title.

Eric Bristow

Born: April 25, 1957 in Hackney, London, England

Major victories: BDO World Champion 1980, 1981, 1984, 1985, 1986
World Masters 1977, 1979, 1981, 1983, 1984

News of the World 1983, 1984
WDF World Cup Singles 1983, 1985, 1987, 1989
WDF World Cup Pairs 1977, 1979, 1983, 1985,1987, 1989
WDF World Cup Team 1979, 1981, 1983, 1987, 1991

The "Crafty Cockney," who took his nickname from a bar he visited in Santa Monica, California, was the first superstar of the professional game, winning five world titles in the 1980s and ruling darts with a confident swagger that at times bordered on arrogance.

"I always felt I would win every tournament I entered," Bristow said of his heyday, and for a period he came close to achieving just that. Bobby George (1980), John Lowe (1981 and 1985), and Dave Whitcombe (1984 and 1986) were his victims in the BDO World Championship final during a seven-year spell in which his superiority was unquestionable.

Bristow also spent seven years as world no. 1 from 1980 to 1987 before disaster struck and he was afflicted by dartitis, a documented psychological problem that prevents a player releasing the dart properly when they attempt to throw.

Bristow bravely fought the condition and returned to play again on the biggest stage, reaching three successive world finals from 1989 to 1991. But defeats by Jocky Wilson, Phil Taylor, and Dennis Priestley signaled the beginning of the end for the most gifted player of his generation.

Taylor, who would go on to eclipse Bristow's feats, was in fact a protégé of the Londoner, who had the foresight to invest £8,000 (approx. $12,000) in backing Taylor when he was an up-and-coming player.

A member of the 1993 breakaway from the BDO, Bristow's final hurrah came four years later when he reached the semi-finals of the PDC World Championship before losing an epic contest in the deciding set, again to Taylor.

Seemingly nerveless on stage, Bristow was the complete opposite—for perhaps the only time—when he was appointed MBE in 1989 for his services to the game. "Meeting the Queen was more nerve-wracking than any TV final I've played in," he said afterward.

2006
Jelle Klaasen becomes the youngest World Champion in the history of darts. The Dutchman, nicknamed "The Matador," is 21 years and 90 days old when he wins the BDO World Championship.

Fact:
Bristow paired up with his great friend and rival John Lowe to win six of the first seven WDF World Cup pairs titles from 1977 to 1989.

Dennis Priestley

Born: July 16, 1950 in Mexborough, South Yorkshire, England

Major victories: BDO World Champion 1991
PDC World Champion 1994
BDO World Masters 1992

In the same way that John Lowe spent much of his career in the shadow of Eric Bristow, so Priestley has been unfortunate to have played at the same time as the greatest player in the game's history, Phil Taylor.

A former coal merchant, the South Yorkshireman had been in the process of purchasing a small newsagent's shop when he claimed his first world title, at his first attempt, by whitewashing Eric Bristow in the 1991 BDO World Championship final.

That victory heralded Priestley's most successful period and he became, statistically, the world's best player from 1991 to 1994, winning three majors during that time.

Within weeks of Priestley being named England captain in 1993, the professional ranks were split between the BDO and PDC and Priestley relinquished the captaincy to join the latter.

He became the new organization's first World Champion in 1994, defeating Taylor in the final. But that was to prove a rare success against Taylor, who went on to defeat Priestley in four world finals between 1996 and 2000.

Although he has not reached a world final since, Priestley remains a leading player. He reached the semi-finals of the 2007 Premier League, a league competition featuring the world's top eight players, and despite battling against prostate cancer, returned to the world's top ten in 2008.

The owner of one of the most consistent throwing actions on the circuit, Priestley is renowned for his professionalism. "It is an underrated requirement," he says. "Some players today still do not conduct themselves in the right manner. They don't practice enough or go the right way about their tournaments. When it comes down to it, there's no substitute for practice.

"Some of the younger players these days beat themselves up during matches. Sometimes you have to ride out the storm and get back to hitting the trebles and doubles. Consistency, of course, is the key requirement. That's why Phil Taylor's still the best there is; he's the most consistent."

Fact:
Priestley is the only player to have won the BDO and PDC World Championships on his first appearance in both tournaments.

2007
In arguably the greatest match in the history of the game, Raymond van Barneveld defeats Phil Taylor 7–6 in the final of the PDC World Championship to become the fourth man to win both the PDC and BDO crowns.

Dennis Priestley

Martin Adams

Born: June 4, 1956, in Sutton, Surrey, England

Major victories: BDO World Champion 2007, 2010
Winmau World Masters 2008, 2009
WDF World Cup Singles 1995, 2001
WDF World Cup Pairs 1995, 2003
World Cup Team 1995, 1999, 2001, 2003, 2007

The Englishman is living proof that a late start need not be a hindrance to success at the top level of the game, having worked for a bank for 22 years before turning professional in 1995.

Adams was 37 when he made his BDO World Championship debut a year earlier and it is testimony to his perseverance that he finally claimed the title at the age of 50.

After losing to Raymond van Barneveld of Holland in the 2005 final, Adams returned two years later to face a fellow 50-year-old, Phill Nixon, from County Durham, in a 2007 showpiece that was one of the most memorable matches in the game's history.

Adams won the first six sets of the best-of-13-sets final but, remarkably, Nixon won the next six to hold a

psychological advantage going into the decider. Adams' wife Sharon had left the arena in tears but her husband recovered his composure to win the set and the championship.

Almost two years later, in December 2008, Adams, at 52, claimed his second major, defeating compatriot Scott Waites by the same scoreline in the Winmau World Masters final. He went on to mount a successful defense of that title 12 months later.

In January 2010, Adams enjoyed another moment of glory when he defeated Dave Chisnall 7–5 in the BDO World Championship final to regain the title.

Having remained with the BDO, Adams, who first played for England in 1990, has been captain for his country since 1993 and remains a firm advocate of the international game. "I still believe international darts is

2008
Anastasia Dobromyslova puts Russia on the darts map by ending Trina Gulliver's winning streak at the BDO World Championship to claim the title.

the best stepping stone for anyone wanting to become professional," he says. "The intensity and pressure is the perfect barometer."

He is also acknowledged as a great ambassador for the game. "I've always been nice to people all the way up," he adds. "It's much easier to be nice to other players, officials, and spectators than nasty and it seems to work. You may be having a bad day but it's best to stay on an even keel. It's like going on stage and putting on a show for people."

Fact:
In 2009, Adams became only the third player successfully to defend the BDO's second major and the game's oldest "world" event, the Winmau World Masters. Bob Anderson (1986 to 1988) and Eric Bristow (1983 and 1984) are the others who achieved the same feat.

Phil Taylor

Champions League 2008
PDC Desert Classic 2002,
  2004, 2005, 2008, 2009 UK
Open 2003, 2005, 2009
PDC UK Matchplay 1996
News of the World
  Championship 1997
WDF World Cup Team 1991

Born: August 13, 1960, in
Burslem, Stoke-on-Trent, England

Major victories: BDO World
  Champion 1990, 1992
BDO Winmau World
  Masters 1990
BDO World Darts Trophy 2006
PDC world champion
  1995, 1996, 1997, 1998,
  1999, 2000, 2001, 2002,
  2004, 2005, 2006, 2009
PDC World Matchplay 1995,
  1997, 2000, 2001,
  2002, 2003, 2004,
  2006, 2008, 2009
World Grand Prix 1998,
  1999, 2000, 2002, 2003
  2005, 2006, 2008
Grand Slam of Darts
  2007, 2008, 2009
PDC Premier League
  2005, 2006, 2007, 2008

Undoubtedly the greatest
player in the history of the
game, Taylor's 2010 World
Championship victory was
the fifteenth world title of his
career (13 PDC, 2 BDO), a
record that most experts
predict will never be beaten.

Taylor was working in a
factory and playing darts
for a pub team when his
talent was spotted by
five-times world champion
Eric Bristow, who became
Taylor's mentor and later,
in 1990 his first victim in a
world final when the relatively
inexperienced 30-year-
old lifted the BDO title.

Living up to his nickname "The Power," Taylor claimed his second BDO world crown the following year before joining the PDC as one of the 16 founding players in 1993. Remarkably, he appeared in the first 14 PDC World Championship finals, winning 11 and losing only to Dennis Priestley (1994), John Part (2003), and Raymond van Barneveld (2007).

Taylor's powers seemed to be waning following his quarter-final defeat by Wayne Mardle in the 2008 World Championship but he silenced his critics by bouncing back to win a fourth successive Premier Darts title, the inaugural Championship League, and a second consecutive Grand Slam of Darts, which pits the best BDO players against the PDC's finest.

In all he won seven major PDC titles in 2008 before regaining his beloved world title by defeating van Barneveld in the 2009 final. His three-dart average score of 110.94 on that occasion was the highest in World Championship history. And in 2010, Taylor rounded off a superb year with another emphatic triumph in the PDC World Championship.

However, Taylor is not one to dwell on past glories: "I've forgotten how many major titles I've won," he says. "You remember the world titles, of course you do, but the others seem to meld into each other. It's all about the next title for me. As soon as I win one, I'm thinking about the next tournament and the one after that. I enjoy the moment but then it's time to move on."

Fact:
Taylor recorded a world record average for a televised event of 116.01 against John Part in their Premier League match in Aberdeen on April 23, 2009.

2009
Barry Hearn, chairman of the PDC, makes an offer to take control of the rival BDO that is rejected out of hand by the organization's founder, Olly Croft.

Raymond van Barneveld

A hugely popular player, the Dutchman emerged as the greatest rival to Phil "The Power" Taylor in the early years of the twenty-first century and is one of only four players to have won both the BDO and PDC World Championships.

Backed by the colorful "Barney Army," his loyal and noisy band of supporters easily identifiable in their orange colors, the Dutchman with the smooth throwing action made steady progress on the BDO circuit before winning the world title in 1998 and 1999, beating Richie Burnett and Ronnie Baxter respectively in dramatic finals that both went to the eleventh and final leg.

Further world titles came in 2003 and 2005, van

Born: April 20, 1967 in The Hague, Netherlands

Major victories: BDO
 World Champion 1998,
 1999, 2003, 2005
PDC World Champion 2007
BDO World Masters
 2001, 2005
BDO World Darts
 Trophy 2003, 2004
BDO International Darts
 League 2003, 2004, 2006
PDC Desert Classic 2007
UK Open 2006, 2007
WDF World Cup Singles
 1997, 1999, 2003

Barneveld accounting for Ritchie Davies and Martin Adams before he suffered a surprise defeat in the 2006 final to 21-year-old compatriot Jelle Klaasen, one of the many Dutch youngsters who had partly been inspired to take up the game by van Barneveld's exploits on the international stage.

Following that defeat, van Barneveld switched codes and joined the PDC, and quickly showed himself to be at home with a nine-dart 501 against Peter Manley in a Premier League match after just a few weeks on the circuit.

Better was to follow as he defeated Taylor in an extraordinary match to win the PDC World Championship at the first attempt in 2007. Van Barneveld hit a world record 21 180s in the final between the two men, which was decided in a sudden-death leg in the thirteenth and final set.

After a surprise early exit the following year, van Barneveld reached the PDC final again in 2009, throwing a nine-dart 501 in his quarter-final victory over Klaasen en route. But he found his friend and rival Taylor in irresistible form. The Englishman won 7–1, leaving van Barneveld to admit he was still playing catch-up with the world no. 1.

"I think there are two important things that have brought me to the top and kept me there," he says. "First of all, I can't stand losing. Reaching a final is not enough; only winning matters. I can't help that; it is just my character. Second, I believe in a professional approach. This sport is more than only throwing a dart. Practice, mental preparation, and physical condition are all vital."

Fact:
Van Barneveld became the first player to hit live televised nine-dart 501s in both the PDC Premier League, 2006 and PDC World Championship 2009.

2010

Phil "The Power" Taylor wins his fifteenth World Championship title when he defeats Australian Simon Whitlock 7–3 in the PDC final at Alexandra Palace in North London. Whitlock, runner-up in the rival BDO Championship two years earlier, has the consolation of setting a record for the number of 180s thrown by one player in the tournament with 58, fifteen more than Taylor.

John Part

Born: June 29, 1966, in
Toronto, Ontario, Canada

Major victories: PDC World
Champion 2003, 2008
BDO World Champion 1994
PDC Desert Classic 2006
WDF World Cup Pairs 1993

Part only began playing
darts seriously as a 21-year-
old but has gone on to
win three world titles and
become the most successful
North American player in
the history of the game.

The Canadian, nicknamed
"Darth Maple," has also
recorded more victories
against Phil Taylor in
major tournaments than
any other player.

Part had never played in
front of the television cameras
before he made his debut at
the BDO World Championship
in 1994, but he swept all
before him to win the title,
whitewashing Bobby George
of England 6–0 in the final

to become the first non-British winner of the title.

However, he was beaten in the second round in each of the following three years and, although he made the switch to the PDC in 1997, it was another four years before he made an impact at the newer organization, reaching the 2001 final only to be defeated by Taylor.

Over the next two years, Part made significant improvements to his game and in 2003 he and Taylor met again in the final. This time Part won 7–6 to end a run of eight successive world title victories by the Englishman and claim the world no. 1 ranking.

In the next five years he won only one televised tournament but in 2008 he claimed his second PDC world title, with victory over Kirk Shepherd of England, making him only the fifth man to win three world crowns after Taylor, Raymond van Barneveld,

John Lowe, and Eric Bristow.

Part has also forged a career as an excellent darts commentator, so it is not surprising that he has an interesting insight into his own career, which has featured many unexpected early exits as well as numerous successes.

"I believe that I am the most dangerously unpredictable player in darts," he says. "Winning three world championships took me 14 years so it is also something that required time and dedication.

"My success in darts is probably due to my competitive nature combined with the philosophy that if you just keep trying eventually you will succeed. It's an outlook that leaves me hopeful of at least one more world title, and of being able to bounce back from any setbacks better than ever."

Fact:
Part was the first man to win world titles at three different venues: the Lakeside in Frimley Green, Surrey (1994), the Circus Tavern in Purfleet, Essex (2003), and Alexandra Palace in North London (2008).

John Part

Ted Hankey

Born: February 20, 1968, in Stoke-on-Trent, England

Major victories: BDO World Champion 2000, 2009

The area of North Staffordshire in England that is known as the Potteries has produced not one but two world champions: Phil Taylor, the greatest player in the history of the game; and Ted "the Count" Hankey, arguably its most memorable stage presence.

Hankey adopted his nickname as a result of having played Dracula in a school play version of the famous gothic novel by Bram Stoker and enters the playing arena dressed in a cape, throwing toy bats to the spectators. While this may be a spot of harmless pre-match fun, the Englishman is a deadly serious competitor, as two world titles testify.

Hankey announced his arrival on the world stage in spectacular fashion at the 2000 BDO World Championship, whitewashing compatriot Ronnie Baxter 6–0 in a final that he finished in style with a 170 checkout in the last leg. Twelve months later, Hankey was back in the final, but this time could manage to win only two sets as another Englishman, John Walton, claimed the title.

Perhaps Hankey's most consistent year came in 2003, when he won the English, Dutch, German, and Danish Open titles. But success at the highest level eluded him for the next few years when, he admitted later, he was not making full use of his undoubted talent. A low point came in 2008, when he was warned by the match referee for punching the dartboard during a quarter-final defeat by Simon Whitlock at the BDO World Championship.

After taking some time out to work on his game though, Hankey—who throws extraordinarily light darts weighing ½ oz (14 g), returned to win his second world title in 2009, defeating his friend and compatriot Tony O'Shea in a rollercoaster final.

Afterwards, an emotional Hankey thanked O'Shea and the other friends on the circuit who had warned him to take things more seriously on and off the oche. "When I won the first title it was great because I always wanted to win it," he said at the time. "But the second win is special. To win it again means more to me for personal reasons."

Ted Hankey

Trina Gulliver

Born: November 30, 1969, in Leamington Spa, Warwickshire, England

Major victories: Women's BDO World Champion 2001, 2002, 2003, 2004, 2005, 2006, 2007, 2010
Women's World Masters 2000, 2002, 2003, 2004, 2005
Women's Las Vegas Desert Classic 2004, 2005
Women's World Darts Trophy 2003
Women's WDF World Cup Singles 1999, 2003
Women's WDF World Cup Pairs 1999, 2003, 2005

The greatest female player in the history of the game, Gulliver, nicknamed "The Golden Girl," has appeared in every BDO Women's World Championship since the event began in 2001, winning seven straight titles before being defeated in the 2008 and 2009 finals, only to regain her crown in 2010.

Five of those victories came against her close friend and rival Francis Hoenselaar of the Netherlands and Gulliver's run of success only ended in 2008, when she was defeated by the new Russian sensation Anastasia Dobromyslova, before Hoenselaar finally exacted a degree of revenge when she beat Gulliver the following year.

Originally a carpenter and joiner by trade, Gulliver has played darts since she was a young child and was representing her county's men's team by the age of 16. Her single-mindedness should ensure that there are many years of success still to come.

"You have to want something badly enough," she says. "Nothing comes for free. Obviously darts is a male-dominated sport but what people don't realize is that there are women's tournaments running in tandem to the main men's events. It just doesn't get the media coverage. You have to have determination and commitment in order to succeed and get to the highest level."

Fact:
In 2003, Gulliver became the first player, male or female, to win the BDO's "Grand Slam" in a calendar year, when she was victorious in the World Championship, World Darts Trophy, World Cup Singles, and Winmau World Masters.

Trina Gulliver

Anastasia Dobromyslova

Born: September 26, 1984, in Tver, Russia

Major victories: BDO World Champion 2008 Women's WDF World Cup Pairs 2007

The glamorous young Russian has already achieved two notable firsts in the game: inflicting a first defeat at the BDO's Women's World Championship on Trina Gulliver in 2008 and becoming the first woman to play alongside the men in the PDC World Championship the following year.

Dobromyslova had won the Russian Championship on six successive occasions, starting in 1999, before she defeated Gulliver on her BDO debut at the Dutch Open in 2004.

She reached the final of the World Darts Trophy later that year before making the semi-finals of the BDO Women's 2007 World Championship on her Lakeside debut.

A year later she returned to take Gulliver's crown and she became the first woman to qualify for the men's UK Open and Grand Slam of Darts in 2008. Her subsequent decision to quit the BDO in order to join the PDC Pro Tour made her the first world champion to fail to defend the women's BDO crown, but it was clear she had her sights set on bigger goals.

"Winning the World Championship was my dream and something I had worked hard for from when I first started to play darts," she says. "My ambitions now are to first of all prove that I can compete against the men and establish myself in the professional game. I am very determined to continue to improve my game and to take myself as far as possible."

Fact:
In the 2009 Grand Slam of Darts Dobromyslova became the first woman to defeat a man in a major televised tournament when she beat Vincent van der Voort of Holland 5–4.

Stacy Bromberg

Born: July 27, 1956,
Los Angeles, California

Major victories: Women's
Las Vegas Desert Classic 2003
WDF World Cup Pairs 1997
WDF World Cup Team 1997
WDF Word Cup Singles 2009

The most successful and
recognizable female in
North American darts,
Bromberg has been the
top-ranked American
woman player since 1996.

Bromberg, who claims she
"stumbled" into the game,

shot to prominence in 1995, reaching the final of the Women's Winmau World Masters only to lose to Sharon Colclough of England.

Two years later she claimed a double success at the World Cup in Perth, Australia, winning the pairs event with her regular partner Lori Verrier and also helping the USA to win the team event.

In 1999, Bromberg was included by *Sports Illustrated* magazine at no. 32 in the top 50 Nevada sports figures of the millennium. She reached the quarter-final of the BDO Women's World Championship in 2002 but her greatest achievement came in 2009 when she won the Women's WDF World Cup Singles title, beating Julie Gore of Wales 7–3 in the final.

Fact:
Bromberg also works as a private investigator in two American states. She is licensed with the Bureau of Consumer Affairs in California and the Attorney General's Office in Nevada.

Stacy Bromberg

Fact:
In 2006,
James Wade hit
a record three
live nine-dart
501s in televised
competition.

James Wade

Born: April 6, 1983, in
Aldershot, England

Major PDC victories:
Premier League 2009
World Matchplay 2007
World Grand Prix 2007
UK Open 2008

A world-class left-hander,
Wade was the PDC Young
Player of the Year in 2006,
when he reached his first
major final at the World
Matchplay just a fortnight
after he had quit his job in
a garage to concentrate
on playing darts full-time.
Twelve months later, he
went one better by claiming
the Matchplay title and his
improvement since then has
taken him as high as no.
2 in the world rankings.

He enjoyed further success
in 2007 when winning the
World Grand Prix, adding
the UK Open in 2008 and
the PDC Premier League,
contested by the world's top
eight players, in 2009. In the
previous season of the last-
named competition, he had
become the first player to beat
Phil Taylor, ending the world
no. 1's run of 44 matches
without defeat. Wade is also
unusual among darts players
in that he has had several
nicknames rather than just
one, including "The Gladiator,"
"009," and "The Machine."

Jelle Klaasen

Born: October 17, 1984,
in Alphen, Netherlands

Major victories: BDO
World Champion 2006

The Dutchman shot to prominence in the darts world in 2006 by becoming the youngest player in the history of the game to win the BDO World Championship.

Klaasen was just 21 when he arrived at the Lakeside Country Club in Surrey as a rank outsider. Armed with a pistol-quick throwing action, he beat Dennis Harbour, Mervyn King, Paul Hogan, and Shaun Greatbatch to reach the final, where he overcome compatriot Raymond van Barneveld by seven sets to five and was immediately earmarked as a star of the future. However, 12 months later he fell at the first hurdle in the defence of his crown to another Dutchman, Co Stompe, and he soon left the BDO to join the PDC. His best performance in the PDC World Championship came in 2009, when he reached the last eight, but he struggled on his debut season in the Premier League, in 2009, finishing eighth and last.

Michael van Gerwen

Born: April 25, 1989, in Boxtel, Netherlands

Major victories: World Masters 2006

A prodigious talent in youth events, van Gerwen stepped up to senior competition in memorable fashion by becoming the youngest player in history to win the World Masters, aged 17 years and 174 days, in October 2006.

That achievement saw him made the favorite for the 2007 BDO World Championship, but he suffered a first-round defeat there. However, he won the Open Holland in 2006 and 2007 before he committed himself to the PDC circuit, on which he has taken some notable scalps, defeating compatriot Raymond van Barneveld in The Players Championship and world no. 1 Phil Taylor in the Masters of Darts tournament. He also came within a dart of defeating Taylor in the 2008 PDC World Championship. Van Gerwen plays under the nickname "Mighty Mike."

Gary Mawson

Born: May 17, 1963 in Etobicoke, Toronto, Canada

Mawson is enjoying his second spell in professional darts, having taken a sabbatical from the game after enjoying a relatively successful "first" career in the late 1990s.

Nicknamed "the Mauler," Mawson made five successive appearances at the PDC World Championship from 1996 to 2000, his best performance coming in 1999 when he reached the last 16.

After a self-imposed five-year exile, when he felt he needed to take a break from the game, he returned to win the 2006 Houston Open. A year later he was selected to represent his adopted country, the USA, at the 2007 WDF World Cup, and the following year saw his best professional performance, when he reached the final of the UK Open only to lose to James Wade of England.

Michael van Gerwen/Gary Mawson

Darin Young

Fact:
Darin Young edged Scott Burnett out of first place in the PDC's North American Order of Merit for 2009 by just $150.

Born: February 2, 1973, in Fairbank, Pennsylvania

The tall left-hander is a genuine all-rounder, having learned his trade playing American Darts, a traditional version of the game in which lightweight wooden darts are thrown, before progressing to the soft-tip and steel-tip games.

Nicknamed "Big Daddy," Young topped the North American Order of Merit as the leading money winner in 2008 and 2009, earning him entry to the PDC World Championship (in which he made his first appearance in 2005) and Grand Slam of Darts in the following year. The best year of his career came in 2008, when he won the North American Darts Championship, Las Vegas Open and, for the third time in his career, the USA Dart Classic. He is also a two-times former winner of the Soft-Tip Bullshooter World Championship, enjoying back-to-back successes in 1999 and 2000.

John Part celebrates his victory at the PDC World Darts Championship final 2008, Alexandra Palace, London.

Chapter Ten: RECORDS

Who was the inaugural world champion? Which player was the first to be crowned king of the world in three different locations? Which female player went on to become a leading sports psychologist? And which Londoner went to America and won a trip to his home town? All the answers and more are in our records section.

PDC World Championship

	Winner	Runner-up
2010	Phil Taylor (England)	Simon Whitlock (Australia)
2009	Phil Taylor (England)	Raymond van Barneveld (Holland)
2008	John Part (Canada)	Kirk Shepherd (England)
2007	Raymond van Barneveld (Holland)	Phil Taylor (England)
2006	Phil Taylor (England)	Peter Manley (England)
2005	Phil Taylor (England)	Mark Dudbridge (England)
2004	Phil Taylor (England)	Kevin Painter (England)
2003	John Part (Canada)	Phil Taylor (England)
2002	Phil Taylor (England)	Peter Manley (England)
2001	Phil Taylor (England)	John Part (Canada)
2000	Phil Taylor (England)	Dennis Priestley (England)
1999	Phil Taylor (England)	Peter Manley (England)
1998	Phil Taylor (England)	Dennis Priestley (England)
1997	Phil Taylor (England)	Dennis Priestley (England)
1996	Phil Taylor (England)	Dennis Priestley (England)
1995	Phil Taylor (England)	Rod Harrington (England)
1994	Dennis Priestley (England)	Phil Taylor (England)

The 2008 final between John Part, of Canada, and Kirk Shepherd, of England, was the first in the history of the PDC World Championship not to feature Phil Taylor, who won eleven and lost three of the first fourteen finals. Shepherd became the youngest player ever to reach the final—he was 21 at the time—and had to win five qualifying matches just to reach the first round. The £50,000 [$80,000] he earned as runner-up was three times more than his career winnings to date at that point.

BDO World Championship

	Winner	**Runner-up**
2010	Martin Adams (England)	Dave Chisnall (England)
2009	Ted Hankey (England)	Tony O'Shea (England)
2008	Mark Webster (Wales)	Simon Whitlock (Australia)
2007	Martin Adams (England)	Phill Nixon (England)
2006	Jelle Klaasen (Holland)	Raymond van Barneveld (Holland)
2005	Raymond van Barneveld (Holland)	Martin Adams (England)
2004	Andy Fordham (England)	Mervyn King (England)
2003	Raymond van Barneveld (Holland)	Richie Davies (Wales)
2002	Tony David (Australia)	Mervyn King (England)
2001	John Walton (England)	Ted Hankey (England)
2000	Ted Hankey (England)	Ronnie Baxter (England)
1999	Raymond van Barneveld (Holland)	Ronnie Baxter (England)
1998	Raymond van Barneveld (Holland)	Richie Burnett (Wales)
1997	Les Wallace (Scotland)	Marshall James (Wales)
1996	Steve Beaton (England)	Richie Burnett (Wales)
1995	Richie Burnett (Wales)	Raymond van Barneveld (Holland)
1994	John Part (Canada)	Bobby George (England)
1993	John Lowe (England)	Alan Warriner-Little (England)
1992	Phil Taylor (England)	Mike Gregory (England)
1991	Dennis Priestley (England)	Eric Bristow (England)
1990	Phil Taylor (England)	Eric Bristow (England)

1989	Jocky Wilson (Scotland)	Eric Bristow (England)
1988	Bob Anderson (England)	John Lowe (England)
1987	John Lowe (England)	Eric Bristow (England)
1986	Eric Bristow (England)	Dave Whitcombe (England)
1985	Eric Bristow (England)	John Lowe (England)
1984	Eric Bristow (England)	Dave Whitcombe (England)
1983	Keith Deller (England)	Eric Bristow (England)
1982	Jocky Wilson (Scotland)	John Lowe (England)
1981	Eric Bristow (England)	John Lowe (England)
1980	Eric Bristow (England)	Bobby George (England)
1979	John Lowe (England)	Leighton Rees (Wales)
1978	Leighton Rees (Wales)	John Lowe (England)

Keith Deller's victory over Eric Bristow in the 1983 BDO World Championship remains one of the greatest achievements in the history of the competition. Deller was the first qualifier to win the tournament and beat the top three players in the world rankings—John Lowe, Jocky Wilson, and Bristow—in the quarter-final, semi-final, and final. His title-winning checkout of 138 in the final has led to a finish on that number being named a "Deller checkout." He works now as a spotter, part of the team covering televised darts events whose job is to help tell the cameramen where the next dart will be thrown.

One of the most remarkable stories in recent years is that of Andy "The Viking" Fordham, who won the 2004 BDO World Championship. Fordham had developed an increasing dependence on alcohol during his career, reportedly consuming 25 bottles of beer before he played, and he weighed over 430 pounds at the time of his world title triumph. Severe health problems ensued and Fordham was forced to take a break from the game, during which he reduced his weight by more than half before returning to action in 2007.

Winmau World Masters

	Winner	Runner-up
2009	Martin Adams (England)	Robbie Green (England)
2008	Martin Adams (England)	Scott Waites (England)
2007	Robert Thornton (Scotland)	Darryl Fitton (England)
2006	Michael van Gerwen (Holland)	Martin Adams (England)
2005	Raymond van Barneveld (Holland)	Goran Klemme (Sweden)
2004	Mervyn King (England)	Tony O'Shea (England)
2003	Tony West (England)	Raymond van Barneveld (Holland)
2002	Mark Dudbridge (England)	Tony West (England)
2001	Raymond van Barneveld (Holland)	Jarkko Komula (Finland)
2000	John Walton (England)	Mervyn King (England)
1999	Andy Fordham (England)	Wayne Jones (England)
1998	Les Wallace (Scotland)	Alan Warriner-Little (England)
1997	Graham Hunt (Australia)	Ronnie Baxter (England)
1996	Colin Monk (England)	Richie Burnett (Wales)
1995	Erik Clarys (Belgium)	Richie Burnett (Wales)
1994	Richie Burnett (Wales)	Steve Beaton (England)
1993	Steve Beaton (England)	Les Wallace (Scotland)
1992	Dennis Priestley (England)	Mike Gregory (England)
1991	Rod Harrington (England)	Phil Taylor (England)
1990	Phil Taylor (England)	Jocky Wilson (Scotland)
1989	Peter Evison (England)	Eric Bristow (England)
1988	Bob Anderson (England)	John Lowe (England)
1987	Bob Anderson (England)	John Lowe (England)
1986	Bob Anderson (England)	Bob Sinnaeve (Canada)
1985	Dave Whitcombe (England)	Ray Farrell (Northern Ireland)
1984	Eric Bristow (England)	Keith Deller (England)
1983	Eric Bristow (England)	Mike Gregory (England)

1982	Dave Whitcombe (England)	Jocky Wilson (Scotland)
1981	Eric Bristow (England)	John Lowe (England)
1980	John Lowe (England)	Rab Smith (Scotland)
1979	Eric Bristow (England)	Allan Hogg (Canada)
1978	Ronnie Davies (Wales)	Tony Brown (England)
1977	Eric Bristow (England)	Paul Reynolds (England)
1976	John Lowe (England)	Phil Obbard (Wales)
1975	Alan Evans (Wales)	David Rocky Jones (Wales)
1974	Cliff Inglis (England)	Harry Heenan (Scotland)

Bob Anderson is the only player to have won the game's oldest major championship three years in succession (1986, 1987, and 1988). "The Limestone Cowboy" was also an England Schools javelin champion and played semi-professional soccer, only for injury to end both careers. After turning to darts, his greatest year came in 1988, when he won the BDO World Championship. He was still ranked in the world's top 32 when he retired at the age of sixty in February 2008.

Professional Darts Corporation

PREMIER LEAGUE

Winner		Runner-up
2009	James Wade (England)	Mervyn King (England)
2008	Phil Taylor (England)	James Wade (England)
2007	Phil Taylor (England)	Terry Jenkins (England)
2006	Phil Taylor (England)	Roland Scholten (Holland)
2005	Phil Taylor (England)	Colin Lloyd (England)

NORTH AMERICAN DARTS CHAMPIONSHIP

Winner		Runner-up
2009	Scotty Burnett (USA)	Darin Young (USA)
2008	Darin Young (USA)	Brad Wethington (USA)

UK OPEN

Winner		Runner-up
2009	Phil Taylor (England)	Colin Osborne (England)
2008	James Wade (England)	Gary Mawson (USA)
2007	Raymond van Barneveld (Holland)	Vincent van der Voort (Holland)
2006	Raymond van Barneveld (Holland)	Barrie Bates (Wales)
2005	Phil Taylor (England)	Mark Walsh (England)
2004	Roland Scholten (Holland)	John Part (Canada)
2003	Phil Taylor (England)	Shayne Burgess (England)

LAS VEGAS DESERT CLASSIC

Winner		Runner-up
2009	Phil Taylor (England)	Raymond van Barneveld (Holland)
2008	Phil Taylor (England)	James Wade (England)
2007	Raymond van Barneveld (Holland)	Terry Jenkins (England)
2006	John Part (England)	Raymond van Barneveld (Holland)
2005	Phil Taylor (England)	Wayne Mardle (England)
2004	Phil Taylor (England)	Wayne Mardle (England)
2003	Peter Manley (England)	John Part (Canada)
2002	Phil Taylor (England)	Ronnie Baxter (England)

WORLD MATCHPLAY

Winner		Runner-up
2009	Phil Taylor (England)	Terry Jenkins (England)
2008	Phil Taylor (England)	James Wade (England)
2007	James Wade (England)	Terry Jenkins (England)
2006	Phil Taylor (England)	James Wade (England)
2005	Colin Lloyd (England)	John Part (Canada)
2004	Phil Taylor (England)	Mark Dudbridge (England)
2003	Phil Taylor (England)	Wayne Mardle (England)
2002	Phil Taylor (England)	John Part (England)
2001	Phil Taylor (England)	Richie Burnett (Wales)
2000	Phil Taylor (England)	Alan Warriner-Little (England)
1999	Rod Harrington (England)	Peter Manley (England)
1998	Rod Harrington (England)	Ronnie Baxter (England)
1997	Phil Taylor (England)	Alan Warriner-Little (England)
1996	Peter Evison (England)	Dennis Priestley (England)
1995	Phil Taylor (England)	Dennis Priestley (England)
1994	Larry Butler (USA)	Dennis Priestley (England)

PLAYERS CHAMPIONSHIP

Winner		Runner-up
2009	Phil Taylor (England)	Robert Thornton (Scotland)

US OPEN

Winner		Runner-up
2009	Dennis Priestley (England)	Andy Hamilton (England)
2008	Phil Taylor (England)	Colin Lloyd (England)
2007	Phil Taylor (England)	Raymond van Barneveld (Holland)

SOUTH AFRICAN MASTERS

Winner		Runner-up
2009	Phil Taylor (England)	James Wade (England)
2008	Phil Taylor (England)	John Part (Canada)
2007	Phil Taylor (England)	Raymond van Barneveld (Holland)

WORLD GRAND PRIX

Winner		Runner-up
2009	Phil Taylor (England)	Raymond van Barneveld (Holland)
2008	Phil Taylor (England)	Raymond van Barneveld (Holland)
2007	James Wade (England)	Terry Jenkins (England)
2006	Phil Taylor (England)	Terry Jenkins (England)
2005	Phil Taylor (England)	Colin Lloyd (England)
2004	Colin Lloyd (England)	Alan Warriner-Little (England)
2003	Phil Taylor (England)	John Part (Canada)
2002	Phil Taylor (England)	John Part (Canada)
2001	Alan Warriner-Little (England)	Roland Scholten (Holland)
2000	Phil Taylor (England)	Shayne Burgess (England)
1999	Phil Taylor (England)	Shayne Burgess (England)
1998	Phil Taylor (England)	Rod Harrington (England)

EUROPEAN CHAMPIONSHIP

Winner		Runner-up
2009	Phil Taylor (England)	Steve Beaton (England)
2008	Phil Taylor (England)	Adrian Lewis (England)

GRAND SLAM OF DARTS

Winner		Runner-up
2009	Phil Taylor (England)	Scott Waites (England)
2008	Phil Taylor (England)	Terry Jenkins (England)
2007	Phil Taylor (England)	Andy Hamilton (England)

GERMAN DARTS CHAMPIONSHIP

Winner		Runner-up
2009	Phil Taylor (England)	Mervyn King (England)
2008	Co Stompe (Holland)	Phil Taylor (England)
2007	Phil Taylor (England)	Denis Ovens (England)

Fact

Dutchman Co Stompe had a three-dart average of 107.28 when he defeated Phil Taylor to win the German Darts Championship in 2008 and claim his first PDC title. Taylor actually had a higher average—108.09 —despite losing to the bespectacled former tram driver, who is nicknamed "The Matchstick" because of his wiry frame and almost bald head.

WDF World Cup

MEN'S SINGLES

2009	Tony O'Shea (England)
2007	Mark Webster (Wales)
2005	Dick van Dijk (Holland)
2003	Raymond van Barneveld (Holland)
2001	Martin Adams (England)
1999	Raymond van Barneveld (Holland)
1997	Raymond van Barneveld (Holland)
1995	Martin Adams (England)
1993	Roland Scholten (Holland)
1991	John Lowe (England)
1989	Eric Bristow (England)
1987	Eric Bristow (England)
1985	Eric Bristow (England)
1983	Eric Bristow (England)
1981	John Lowe (England)
1979	Nicky Virachkul (USA)
1977	Leighton Rees (Wales)

Nicky Virachkul, the 1979 World Cup men's singles champion, was one of the first American players to enjoy success on the world stage. Born in Thailand but educated in New York, Virachkul began playing the game when he worked in a bar and went on to represent the United States and appear in the BDO World Championship eight times, finishing third in the first tournament in 1978 and famously defeating the defending champion Keith Deller in the first round in 1984. Virachkul died in 1999.

MEN'S PAIRS

2009	Anthony Fleet and Geoff Kime (Australia)
2007	Mario Robbe and Joey ten Berge (Holland)
2005	Raymond van Barneveld and Vincent van der Voort (Holland)
2003	Martin Adams and Mervyn King (England)
2001	Andy Fordham and John Walton (England)
1999	Ritchie Davies and Richie Herbert (Wales)
1997	Sean Palfrey and Martin Phillips (Wales)
1995	Martin Adams and Andy Fordham (England)

1993	John Part and Carl Mercer (Canada)
1991	Keith Sullivan and Wayne Weening (Australia)
1989	Eric Bristow and John Lowe (England)
1987	Eric Bristow and John Lowe (England)
1985	Eric Bristow and John Lowe (England)
1983	Eric Bristow and John Lowe (England)
1981	Cliff Lazarenko and Tony Brown (England)
1979	Eric Bristow and John Lowe (England)
1977	Eric Bristow and John Lowe (England)

OVERALL WINNERS

2009	Holland	1999	England	1989	England	1979	England
2007	Holland	1997	Wales	1987	England	1977	Wales
2005	Holland	1995	England	1985	England		
2003	England	1993	Wales	1983	England		
2001	England	1991	England	1981	England		

MEN'S TEAM EVENT

2009	Holland (Joey ten Berge, Willy van der Wiel, Frans Harmsen, Daniel Brouwer)
2007	England (Martin Adams, Steve Farmer, Tony O'Shea, John Walton)
2005	Finland (Jarkko Komula, Ulf Ceder, Marko Pusa, Kim Viljanen)
2003	United States (Ray Carver, John Kuczynski, Bill Davis, George Walls)
2001	England (Martin Adams, Andy Fordham, Mervyn King, John Walton)
1999	England (Ronnie Baxter, Martin Adams, Andy Fordham, Mervyn King)
1997	Wales (Eric Burden, Marshall James, Sean Palfrey, Martin Phillips)
1995	England (Steve Beaton, Ronnie Baxter, Martin Adams, Andy Fordham)
1993	England (Steve Beaton, Ronnie Baxter, Kevin Kenny, Dave Askew)
1991	England (Eric Bristow, John Lowe, Phil Taylor, Alan Warriner)
1989	Canada (Bob Sinnaeve, Rick Bisaro, Tony Holyoak, Albert Anstey)
1987	England (Eric Bristow, John Lowe, Cliff Lazarenko, Bob Anderson)
1985	United States (Tony Payne, Rick Ney, John Kramer, Dan Valletto)
1983	England (Eric Bristow, John Lowe, Keith Deller, Dave Whitcombe)
1981	England (Eric Bristow, John Lowe, Tony Brown, Cliff Lazarenko)
1979	England (Eric Bristow, John Lowe, Tony Brown, Bill Lennard)
1977	Wales (Leighton Rees, Alan Evans, David Jones)

ANTWERP OPEN

2009	Ian White (England)
2008	Andy Hamilton (England)
2007	Terry Jenkins (England)
2006	Terry Jenkins (England)
2005	Terry Jenkins (England)
2004	Colin Lloyd (England)
2003	Colin Lloyd (England)
2002	Colin Lloyd (England)
2001	Martin Adams (England)
2000	Jamie Harvey (Scotland)
1999	Mervyn King (England)
1998	Phil Taylor (England)
1997	Phil Taylor (England)
1996	Bob Anderson (England)
1995	Dennis Priestley (England)
1994	Dennis Priestley (England)
1993	Mike Gregory (England)
1992	Jef van Heertum (Belgium)
1991	Stefan Eeckelaert (Belgium)
1990	Leo Laurens (Belgium)
1989	Steve Brown (USA)
1988	Steve Brown (USA)

AUSTRALIAN MASTERS

2009	Andy Robertson (Australia)
2008	Eddy Sims (Australia)
2007	Simon Whitlock (Australia)
2006	Simon Whitlock (Australia)
2005	Joe Comito (Australia)
2004	Scott Krause (Australia)
2003	Simon Whitlock (Australia)
2002	Simon Whitlock (Australia)
2001	Tony David (Australia)
2000	Tony David (Australia)
1999	Wayne Weening (Australia)
1998	Graham Hunt (Australia)
1997	Steve Duke Sr (Australia)
1996	Tony David (Australia)
1995	Darren Webster (Australia)
1994	Peter Hinkley (Australia)
1993	Frank Tarr (Australia)
1992	Dennis Priestley (England)
1991	Wayne Atkins (Australia)
1990	Ian Findlayson (Australia)
1989	Wayne Weening (Australia)
1988	Russell Stewart (Australia)
1987	Russell Stewart (Australia)
1986	Brian Bigham (Australia)
1985	Russell Stewart (Australia)
1984	Russell Stewart (Australia)
1983	Russell Stewart (Australia)
1982	Frank Palko (Australia)
1981	Andy Robinson (Australia)
1980	Andy Robinson (Australia)
1979	Brian Bigham (Australia)

AUSTRALIAN GRAND MASTERS

2009	Anthony Fleet (Australia)
2008	Tony David (Australia)
2007	Simon Whitlock (Australia)
2006	Simon Whitlock (Australia)
2005	Simon Whitlock (Australia)
2004	Simon Whitlock (Australia)
2003	Peter Hunt (Australia)
2002	Tony David (Australia)
2001	Russell Stewart (Australia)
2000	Peter Hinkley (Australia)
1999	Steve Duke Snr (Australia)
1998	Steve Duke Snr (Australia)
1997	Peter Hinkley (Australia)
1996	Peter Hinkley (Australia)
1995	Wayne Atkins (Australia)
1994	Wayne Atkins (Australia)
1993	Russell Stewart (Australia)
1992	Mike Gregory (England)
1991	Keith Sullivan (Australia)
1990	Russell Stewart (Australia)
1989	Russell Stewart (Australia)
1988	Russell Stewart (Australia)
1987	Russell Stewart (Australia)
1986	Mike Gregory (England)
1985	John Lowe (England)
1984	Horrie Seden (Australia)
1983	Paul Lim (USA)

BELGIUM OPEN

2009	John Henderson (Scotland)
2008	Scott Waites (England)
2007	Tony West (England)
2006	Darryl Fitton (England)
2005	Albertino Essers (Holland)
2004	Willem Kralt (Holland)
2003	Tony West (England)
2002	Ted Hankey (England)
2001	John Walton (England)
2000	Co Stompe (England)
1999	Raymond van Barneveld (Holland)
1998	Martin Adams (England)
1997	Martin Adams (England)
1996	Raymond van Barneveld (Holland)
1995	Mike Gregory (England)
1994	Mike Gregory (England)
1993	Steve Beaton (England)
1992	Rod Harrington (England)
1991	Rod Harrington (England)
1990	Alan Warriner-Little (England)
1989	Alan Warriner-Little (England)
1988	Frans Devooght (Belgium)
1987	Kurt Dumarey (Belgium)
1986	Don Dillon (England)
1985	Don Dillon (England)
1984	Ritchie Gardner (England)
1983	Willy Sonneville (Belgium)
1982	Gustaaf de Meulemeester (Belgium)

BRITISH CLASSIC

2009	Stephen Bunting (England)
2008	Ross Montgomery (Scotland)
2007	Co Stompe (Holland)
2006	Gary Anderson (Scotland)
2005	Paul Hogan (England)

2004	Darryl Fitton (England)
2003	Mark Foreman (England)
2002	Mervyn King (England)
2001	John Walton (England)
2000	Richie Davies (Wales)
1999	Mervyn King (England)
1998	Mervyn King (England)
1997	Dennis Priestley (England)

BRITISH OPEN

2009	Dave Chisnall (England)
2008	John Henderson (Scotland)
2007	Gary Anderson (Scotland)
2006	Mick Reed (England)
2005	Brian Sorensen (Denmark)
2004	Martin Adams (England)
2003	Darryl Fitton (England)
2002	Tony Eccles (England)
2001	John Walton (England)
2000	Mervyn King (England)
1999	Raymond van Barneveld (Holland)
1998	Colin Monk (England)
1997	Kevin Painter (England)
1996	Roland Scholten (Holland)
1995	Al Hedman (England)
1994	Martin Adams (England)
1993	Dennis Priestley (England)
1992	Phil Gilman (England)
1991	Mike Gregory (England)
1990	Alan Warriner-Little (England)
1989	Brian Cairns (Wales)
1988	John Lowe (England)
1987	Bob Anderson (England)
1986	Eric Bristow (England)

1985	John Cosnett (England)
1984	Cliff Lazarenko (England)
1983	Eric Bristow (England)
1982	Jocky Wilson (Scotland)
1981	Eric Bristow (England)
1980	Cliff Lazarenko (England)
1979	Tony Brown (England)
1978	Eric Bristow (England)
1977	John Lowe (England)
1976	Jack North (England)
1975	Alan Evans (Wales)

CANADIAN OPEN

2009	Jerry Hull (Canada)
2008	Jerry Hull (Canada)
2007	Mark Webster (Wales)
2006	John DeGrunchy (Canada)
2005	Dan Olsen (Canada)
2004	John Part (Canada)
2003	Marcel Simard (Canada)
2002	Marcel Simard (Canada)
2001	John Part (Canada)
2000	Peter Manley (England)
1999	Matt Clark (England)
1998	Raymond van Barneveld
1997	Shawn Brenneman (Canada)
1996	Carl Mercer (Canada)
1995	John Part (Canada)
1994	Dennis Priestley (England)
1993	Dennis Priestley (England)
1992	Bob Anderson (England)
1991	Mike Gregory (England)
1990	Bob Anderson (England)
1989	John Lowe (England)
1988	Phil Taylor (England)

1987	John Lowe (England)
1986	John Lowe (England)
1985	Rick Bisaro (Canada)

DENMARK OPEN

2009	Ian White (England)
2008	Krzysztof Ratajski (Poland)
2007	Steve West (England)
2006	Vincent van der Voort (Holland)
2005	Shaun Greatbatch (England)
2004	Gary Anderson (Scotland)
2003	Ted Hankey (England)
2002	Vincent van der Voort (Holland)
2001	Wayne Mardle (England)
2000	Martin Adams (England)
1999	Peter Johnstone (Scotland)
1998	Rod Harrington (England)
1997	Raymond van Barneveld (Holland)
1996	Ronnie Baxter (England)
1995	Colin Monk (England)
1994	Richie Burnett (Wales)
1993	Steve Beaton (England)
1992	Rod Harrington (England)
1991	Rod Harrington (England)
1990	Phil Taylor (England)
1989	Eric Bristow (England)
1988	Dave Askew (England)
1987	John Lowe (England)
1986	Bob Anderson (England)
1985	John Lowe (England)

1984	Eric Bristow (England)
1983	Cliff Lazarenko (England)
1982	John Lowe (England)
1981	Cliff Lazarenko (England)
1980	Eric Bristow (England)
1979	John Lowe (England)
1978	John Lowe (England)
1977	Stefan Lord (Sweden)
1976	Martin Humphrey (England)
1975	Alf Jeffries (Wales)
1974	Bill Geary (England)

DUTCH OPEN

2009	Darryl Fitton (England)
2008	Robert Thornton (England) (Scotland)
2007	Scott Waites (England)
2006	Raymond van Barneveld (Holland)
2005	Tony Eccles (England)
2004	Raymond van Barneveld (Holland)
2003	Ted Hankey (England)
2002	Shaun Greatbatch (England)
2001	Raymond van Barneveld (Holland)
2000	Wayne Mardle (England)
1999	Ted Hankey (England)
1998	Alan Warriner-Little (England)
1997	Mervyn King (England)
1996	Steve Beaton (England)
1995	Steve Beaton (England)
1994	Richie Burnett (Wales)
1993	Alan Warriner-Little
1992	Leo Laurens (Belgium)
1991	Kosta Iauassas (Greece)

1990	Leo Laurens (Belgium)
1989	Alan Warriner-Little
1988	Steve Brown (USA)
1987	Bob Renard (Belgium)
1986	Lee Topper (England)
1985	Frans Devooght (Belgium)
1984	Frans Devooght (Belgium)
1983	Luc Marreel (Belgium)
1982	Jilles Vermaat (Holland)
1981	Gordon Watson (England)
1980	Brian Fenby (England)
1979	Daniel Serie (Belgium)
1978	Jimmy Cox (Holland)
1977	Peter Smith (England)
1976	Henk van Tuijl (Holland)
1975	Terry Henney (England)
1974	Mary de Knoop (Holland)
1973	Ton Koster (Holland)

ENGLAND OPEN

2009	Ted Hankey (England)
2008	Ross Montgomery (Scotland)
2007	Ted Hankey (England)
2006	Mike Veitch (Scotland)
2005	Tony Eccles (England)
2004	Dave Routledge (England)
2003	Ted Hankey (England)
2002	Brian Derbyshire (England)
2001	Chris Mason (England)
2000	Andy Jenkins (England)
1999	Peter Manley (England)
1998	Alan Warriner-Little (England)
1997	Andy Smith (England)

1996	Geoff Wylie (Northern Ireland)
1995	Kevin Painter (England)

FINNISH OPEN

2009	Robert Wagner (Norway)
2008	Steve West (England)
2007	Dietmar Burger (Austria)
2006	Martin Atkins (England)
2005	Marko Pusa (Finland)
2004	Raymond van Barneveld (Holland)
2003	Co Stompe (Holland)
2002	Martin Adams (England)
2001	Bob Taylor (Scotland)
2000	Mervyn King (England)
1999	Paul Williams (England)
1998	Ronnie Baxter (England)
1997	Mervyn King (England)
1996	Martin Adams (England)
1995	Raymond van Barneveld (Holland)
1994	Andy Fordham (England)
1993	Alan Warriner-Little (England)
1992	John Lowe (England)
1991	Per Skau (Denmark)
1990	Phil Taylor (England)
1989	Steve Gittins (England)
1988	Peter Evison (England)
1987	Mike Gregory (England)
1986	Jocky Wilson (Scotland)
1985	Dave Whitcombe (England)
1984	Mike Gregory (England)
1983	Tapani Uitos (Finland)
1981	Kexi Heinaharjo (Finland)

FRENCH OPEN

2009	Ronald L. Briones (Philippines)
2008	Mareno Michels (Holland)
2007	Dennis te Kloese (Holland)
2006	Ron Meulenkamp (Holland)
2005	Dominique le Roy (France)
2003	Tony David (Australia)
2002	Martin Adams (England)
2001	Chris van den Bergh (Belgium)
2000	Olivier Spreutels (Belgium)
1999	Peter Evison (England)
1998	Peter Manley (England)
1997	Peter Evison (England)
1996	Mervyn King (England)
1995	Pascal Rabau (Belgium)
1994	Vijay Kumar (England)
1993	Rod Harrington (England)
1992	Leo Laurens (Belgium)
1991	Rod Harrington (England)
1990	Stefan Eeckelaert (Belgium)
1989	Dave Askew (England)

GERMAN OPEN

2009	John Henderson (Scotland)
2008	Gary Anderson (Scotland)
2007	Martin Adams (England)
2006	Gary Anderson (Scotland)
2005	Paul Hanvidge (Scotland)
2004	Gary Anderson (Scotland)
2003	Ted Hankey (England)
2002	Ted Hankey (England)
2001	Martin Adams (England)
2000	Shayne Burgess (England)
1999	Steve Coote (England)
1998	Alan Warriner-Little (England)
1997	Pascal Lefevre (Belgium)
1996	Colin Monk (England)
1995	Ronnie Baxter (England)
1994	Per Skau (Denmark)
1993	Peter Evison (England)
1992	Peter Evison (England)
1991	Bruno Raes (Belgium)
1990	Kai Pfeiffer (Germany)
1986	Bernd Hebecker (Germany)

NORTH AMERICAN OPEN DARTS TOURNAMENT

2000	Luis Martinez (USA)
1999	John Kramer (USA)
1998	Brad Wethington (USA)
1997	Peter Manley (England)
1996	Roger Carter (USA)
1995	Rudy Hernandez (USA)
1994	Kevin Spiolek (England)
1993	Bob Anderson (England)
1992	Alan Warriner-Little (England)
1991	Phil Taylor (England)
1990	Phil Taylor (England)
1989	Steve Brown (USA)
1988	Steve Brown (USA)
1987	John Lowe (England)
1986	Eric Bristow (England)
1985	John Lowe (England)
1984	Eric Bristow (England)
1983	Eric Bristow (England)
1982	Nicky Virachkul (USA)
1981	John Kramer (USA)
1980	Len Heard (USA)
1979	Eric Bristow (England)
1978	Bobby George (England)
1977	Alan Glazier (England)

1976	Ricky Fusco (England)
1975	Conrad Daniels (USA)
1974	Joe Baltadonis (USA)
1973	Ray Fischer (USA)
1972	Ray Fischer (USA)
1971	Bob Thiede (USA)
1970	Vince Lubbering (USA)

SCOTTISH OPEN

2009	Tony O'Shea (England)
2008	Garry Thompson (England)
2007	Gary Anderson (Scotland)
2006	Goran Klemme (Sweden)
2005	Martin Adams (England)
2004	Mike Veitch (Scotland)
2003	Davy Richardson (England)
2002	Richie Davies (Wales)
2001	John Walton (England)
2000	Bob Aldous (England)
1999	Denis Ovens (England)
1998	Peter Johnstone (Scotland)
1997	Bob Arrowsmith (England)
1996	Mark Salmon (Wales)
1995	Chris Mason (England)
1983	Russell Stewart (Australia)

SWEDISH OPEN

2009	Willy van de Wiel (Holland)
2008	Scott Waites (England)
2007	Shaun Greatbatch (England)
2006	Tony Eccles (England)
2005	Tony Eccles (England)
2004	Shaun Greatbatch (England)
2003	Raymond van Barneveld (Holland)
2002	Raymond van Barneveld (Holland)
2001	Stefan Nagy (Sweden)
2000	Kevin Painter (England)
1999	Erik Clarys (Belgium)
1998	Raymond van Barneveld (Holland)
1997	Richie Davies (Wales)
1996	Roland Scholten (Holland)
1995	Wayne Weening (Australia)
1994	Eric Burden (Wales)
1993	Per Skau (Denmark)
1992	Mike Gregory (England)
1991	Rod Harrington (England)
1990	Dave Whitcombe (England)
1989	Mike Gregory (England)
1988	Steve Gittins (England)
1987	Dave Whitcombe (England)
1986	Bob Anderson (England)
1985	Dave Whitcombe (England)
1984	Bjorn Enqvist (Sweden)
1982	Eric Bristow (England)
1981	Eric Bristow (England)
1980	Tony Sontag (England)
1979	Eric Bristow (England)
1978	Alan Glazier (England)
1977	Bill Perry (England)
1976	Bill Lennard (England)
1975	Bill Perry (England)
1974	Peter Chapman (England)
1973	Kim Brown (England)
1972	Brian Netherton (England)
1971	Tom Barrett (England)
1970	Tom Barrett (England)
1969	Barry Twomlow (England)

USA DART CLASSIC

2009   Jerry van Loan (USA)
2006   David Marienthal (USA)
2008   Darin Young (USA)
2005   Darin Young (USA)
2007   Larry Butler (USA)
2004   Darin Young (USA)

WELSH OPEN

2009   Ross Montgomery (Scotland)
2008   Gary Anderson (Scotland)
2007   Mark Webster (Wales)
2006   Michael van Gerwen (Holland)
2005   Per Laursen (Denmark)
2004   Anthony Ridler (Wales)
2003   Ian Brand (England)
2002   Andy Fordham (England)
2001   Gary Anderson (Scotland)
2000   John Walton (England)
1999   Andy Smith (England)
1998   Steve Alker (Wales)
1997   Marshall James (Wales)
1996   Nicky Turner (England)
1995   Richie Burnett (Wales)
1994   Richie Burnett (Wales)
1993   Ronnie Baxter (England)
1992   Dennis Priestley (England)
1991   Ronnie Baxter (England)
1990   Kevin Kenny (England)
1989   Chris Dalton (England)
1988   Steve Gittins (England)

BDO WOMEN'S WORLD CHAMPIONSHIP

Winner		Runner-up
2010	Trina Gulliver (England)	Rhian Edwards (Wales)
2009	Francis Hoenselaar (Holland)	Trina Gulliver (England)
2008	Anastasia Dobromyslova (Russia)	Trina Gulliver (England)
2007	Trina Gulliver (England)	Francis Hoenselaar (Holland)
2006	Trina Gulliver (England)	Francis Hoenselaar (Holland)
2005	Trina Gulliver (England)	Francis Hoenselaar (Holland)
2004	Trina Gulliver (England)	Francis Hoenselaar (Holland)
2003	Trina Gulliver (England)	Anne Kirk (Scotland)
2002	Trina Gulliver (England)	Francis Hoenselaar (Holland)
2001	Trina Gulliver (England)	Mandy Solomonds (England)

WINMAU WORLD MASTERS – WOMEN

Winner		Runner-up
2009	Linda Ithurralde (England)	Trina Gulliver (England)
2008	Francis Hoenselaar (Holland)	Anastasia Dobromyslova (Russia)
2007	Karin Krappen (England)	Karen Lawman (England)
2006	Francis Hoenselaar (Holland)	Karin Krappen (England)
2005	Trina Gulliver (England)	Francis Hoenselaar (Holland)
2004	Trina Gulliver (England)	Francis Hoenselaar (Holland)
2003	Trina Gulliver (England)	Crissy Manley (England)
2002	Trina Gulliver (England)	Karen Lawman (England)
2001	Anne Kirk (Scotland)	Marilyn Popp (USA)
2000	Trina Gulliver (England)	Francis Hoenselaar (Holland)
1999	Francis Hoenselaar (Holland)	Trina Gulliver (England)
1998	Karen Lawman (England)	Trina Gulliver (England)
1997	Mandy Solomonds (England)	Sandra Greatbatch (Wales)
1996	Sharon Douglas (Scotland)	Heike Ernst (Germany)
1995	Sharon Colclough (England)	Stacy Bromberg (England)
1994	Deta Hedman (England)	Mandy Solomonds (England)
1993	Mandy Solomonds (England)	Kathy Maloney (USA)
1992	Leeanne Maddock (Wales)	Sandra Greatbatch (Wales)
1991	Sandy Reitan (USA)	Hege Lokken (Norway)
1990	Rhian Speed (Wales)	Deta Hedman (England)

1989	Mandy Solomonds (England)	Sharon Colclough (England)
1988	Mandy Solomonds (England)	Maureen Flowers (England)
1987	Ann Thomas (Wales)	Cathie McCulloch (Scotland)
1986	Kathy Wones (England)	Jayne Kempster (England)
1985	Lilian Barnett (New Zealand)	Sonja Ralphs (England)
1984	Kathy Wones (England)	Sandy Earnshaw (England)
1983	Sonja Ralphs (England)	Lil Coombes (England)
1982	Ann Marie Davies (Wales)	Maureen Flowers (England)

WDF WORLD CUP—SINGLES

2009	Stacy Bromberg (USA)	1995	Mandy Solomons (England)
2007	Jan Robbins (USA)	1993	Kathy Maloney (USA)
2005	Clare Bywaters (England)	1991	Jill McDonald (Australia)
2003	Trina Gulliver (England)	1989	Eva Grigsby (USA)
2001	Francis Hoenselaar (Holland)	1987	Valery Maytum (Holland)
1999	Trina Gulliver (England)	1985	Linda Batten (England)
1997	Noeline Gear (Australia)	1983	Sandy Reitan (USA)

NORTH AMERICAN OPEN DARTS TOURNAMENT

2000	Stacy Bromberg (USA)	1983	Judy Campbell (England)
1999	Stacy Bromberg (USA)	1982	Angie Burns (England)
1998	Stacy Bromberg (USA)	1981	Maureen Flowers (England)
1997	Stacy Bromberg (USA)	1980	Sandra Gibb (Wales)
1996	Stacy Bromberg (USA)	1979	Maureen Flowers (England)
1995	Stacy Bromberg (USA)	1978	Kathy Karpowich (USA)
1994	Barbara Barnes (USA)	1977	Maureen Flowers (England)
1992	Mandy Solomons (England)	1976	Donna Dertadian (USA)
1990	Mandy Solomons (England)	1975	Julie Nicoll (USA)
1989	Mandy Solomons	1974	Helen Scheerbaum (USA)
1987	Connie Sroka (USA)	1973	Carol Toulson (USA)
1986	Kathy Maloney (USA)	1972	Gerry McCarthy (USA)
1985	Kathy Maloney (USA)	1971	Gerry McCarthy (USA)
1984	Kathy Karpowich (USA)	1970	Robbi Dobbs (USA)

Fact

After she finished playing at the top level, Englishwoman Linda Batten, the WDF World Cup women's singles champion in 1985 (now Dr Linda Duffy), became a sport and exercise psychologist and now works at Middlesex University. Her research degree was "Gender Differences in Target-throwing Skills and Dart-playing Performance: Evidence from Elite Dart Players" and she has since worked with many leading throwers, including the world No.1, Phil Taylor.

WDF Rules and Regulations

THROW

- Players shall provide their own darts, which shall not exceed an overall length of 12in. (30.5 cm) nor weigh more than $1\frac{3}{4}$ oz (50 g). Each dart shall consist of a needle shaped point which shall be fixed to a barrel. At the rear of the barrel there shall be attached a flighted stem, which may consist of up to five separate pieces. (e.g.: a flight, a flight securing device(s), a flight protector, and a stem.)

- All darts shall be thrown deliberately, one at a time, by and from the hand. All darts must be thrown with the needlepoint aimed towards the face of the dartboard. If a dart is not thrown in this manner then the "throw" will be declared a "foul throw" and will not count in that respective leg, set, or match.

- A throw shall consist of a maximum of "three" darts.

- If a player, during a throw, touches any dart that is in the dartboard, then that throw shall be deemed to have been completed.

- Any dart bouncing off or falling out of the dartboard shall not be thrown again.

- Any dart falling out of the dartboard before the throw has been completed and the darts retrieved shall not count.

- A player deliberately abusing the dartboard when retrieving darts at the end of a throw will be given a verbal warning by the match referee. Another warning will be given if a second incident occurs in the same match. If a third incident occurs in the same match then the player in question will forfeit that respective leg, or set, match.

STARTING AND FINISHING

- Each match or Leg shall be played with a straight start. i.e.: to begin scoring the player need only land a dart in the dartboard inside the outer Doubles wire of the dartboard. Each match or Leg shall be played with a double finish. i.e.: to finish, and win, the player must land a dart in the double (Double Ring or Bull) of the number equal to one half of the remaining score.

- The Bull shall count as "50" and if the score of "50" is required to complete a Leg or match, the Bull shall count as double "25."

- The Bust Rule shall apply. i.e.: if a player in a throw scores more points than remain in the Leg or match, or the same points as remain without finishing on a double, or leaves a score of one, then that throw shall not count and the score shall remain as it was prior to that throw.

- A "Game Shot" called by a Caller is valid only if the darts thrown achieve the required finish and remain in the dartboard until retrieved after the "Game Shot" has been called.

- If a "Game Shot" called by a Caller is invalid, then the player shall have the right to continue that throw. i.e.: If all three darts have not already been thrown.

- If the player has retrieved any of the darts and not all three darts have been thrown, then the Referee shall replace the retrieved dart or darts in as near as is practicable the same position and permit the player to complete the throw.

- The first player who finishes by obtaining the required double out shall be declared the winner of that Leg or match, whichever is applicable.

- A dart thrown by a player after finishing shall not count.

- In a match, or Set divided into Legs, the match or Set shall be played "best of three" (five, seven, etc.) Legs. e.g.: the first player that wins a majority of the given number of legs shall be the winner of the match or Set and the remaining Legs, if any, shall not be played.

- In a match divided into Sets, the match shall be played "best of three" (five, seven, etc.) sets; e.g.: the first player who wins a majority of the given number of Sets shall be the winner of the match and the remaining Sets, if any, shall not be played.

SCORING

- The rules of the event shall provide for matches or Legs of a fixed odd number, such as 501, 701, or 1001. All scores made shall be subtracted

from the given total or the score remaining from the previous throw.

- A dart shall only score if the point remains in or touches the face of the dartboard, within the outer double wire, until after the throw has been completed, and the score has been called and recorded on the scoreboard.

- The score is counted from the side of the segment wire in which the point of the dart enters or touches the face of the dartboard.

- Darts shall be retrieved from the dartboard by the thrower, excepting only in those circumstances when a physical disability, or physical injury requires a player to have assistance, but only after the score has been announced by the Referee, and recorded by the Marker.

- A protest about the score attained, or called, after the retrieval of the darts shall not be upheld.

- Errors in arithmetic shall stand as written on the scoreboard unless corrected prior to the next throw of the player whose score is in error.

- The actual score required by a player must be shown on the scoreboard, clearly visible, at eye level, in front of the players and the Referee.

- No indication of the required "double out" shall be given by the Referee, Caller, Marker, or Scorer. e.g.: "32" not "double 16."

The Referee shall act as an umpire in all matters pertaining to the Playing Rules when conducting a darts match and shall, if necessary, consult with Scorers and other Officials before announcing any decisions during the course of matchplay.

Index

Main references to players are indicated in bold type.

The Darts Bible